Ford, you can finance it with Ford**Credit** - the flexible way to finance your Ford.
Two choices to consider are :

1. Ford

Ford**Opt**
to enjoy a
offers you
Minimum
protects y
in used ca
your repa
vehicle va
deposit yo

At the end
choose fro
a new car
car, or if th
within the
return the

2. Ford

This is the
financing
convenien
terms to s
an initial de
spread the
interest ch
allowing yo
repaymen
end of the
Ford car o

Feel safe with Ford Insure****

Of course, once you have purc
your new Ford you'll
Ford**Insure** offers ne

range of great value products for you and your Ford including Comprehensive Motor Insurance, Payment Protection
otection.
wners,
motor
and
at value,
, benefits

ce offers
r Ford
tarts at 2E.

arranty/

nties for
esigned to
owning
plan
onfident
rs

est dealer
enjoy the
overing
spare

ould put
y. Visit
7 111 888
for more information.

Ford

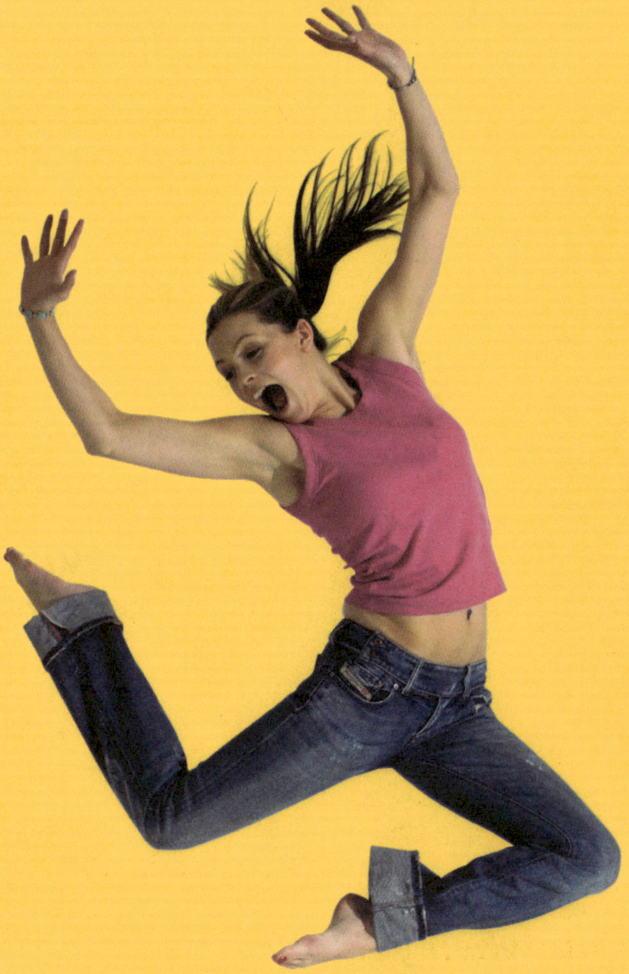

How do I get a free driving lesson?

Supervising a Learner Driver

by Huw Dunley
BA, PGCE, ADI

AA Publishing

Written by Huw Dunley
Consultant editors Sue Hubbard, Shaun Thompson

Images courtesy of AA World Travel Library:
J Beazley 70/1; C Jones 87; J Holmes 40/1;
J McMillan 14/5; J A Tims 8/9, 12/3, 21, 24/5, 30/1,
49, 61, 67, 72/3, 75, 83, 85, 91; W Voysey 53;
R Weir 95; L Whitwam 44/5; P Wilson 18/9.
Digitalvision: 27, 79

Produced by AA Publishing

ISBN-10: 0-7495-4541-0
ISBN-13: 9780-7495-4541-3

Published by AA Publishing (a trading name of Automobile Association Developments Limited, whose registered office is Southwood East, Apollo Rise, Farnborough, Hampshire GU14 0JW; registered number 1878835).

A02358

Colour separation by KDP Ltd
Printed in Spain by Graficas Estella

The AA's website address is
www.theAA.com/bookshop

Contents

Introduction

Helping someone to learn to drive is one of the most stressful and frightening experiences you are likely to encounter during your life. Many years ago, well before I became a driving instructor, I taught my wife to drive. Apart from the number of rows, the shouting and slamming of doors and so on, the whole experience was pretty horrific. Only a driver can appreciate just how difficult it is to sit in the passenger's seat while some incompetent does their utmost to strip every tooth off every cog in every gear; to watch a wall approaching, knowing that you are incapable of stopping the car; to endure the derision of every other driver when your learner stalls in the middle of a crossroads.

It needn't be like that. With the benefit of hindsight and subsequent years of training, practice and experience as a professional driving instructor, I now recognise that it was not my wife's driving that was the problem. Rather, it was my lack of knowledge and skill in clearly communicating what I wanted her to do.

This book is not intended to turn you into a driving instructor, but it is intended to help you support the work that your learner's instructor has done. **There is no substitute for proper professional instruction.** It is unlikely that you will find yourself in the position of being able to teach a learner, but with the aid of this book you will be in a position to make practice sessions useful and enjoyable.

Requirements

If you are to accompany a learner driver then you must be at least 21 years old and have held a full driving licence for at least 3 years. You are not allowed to receive any payment, either monetary or in kind, unless you are an Approved Driving Instructor (ADI), neither may you accept money for fuel.

The car must be taxed and insured for use by the learner and yourself and, if over three years old, must have a valid MOT certificate. It must be fitted with regulation sized L-plates (or D-plates if driven in Wales), which are positioned so that they can be clearly seen from both the front and rear without obstructing the driver's vision (do not place them in the front or rear windows). When the car is not being driven by a learner, the L-plates must be removed or covered up.

Although this is not a legal requirement, it is essential that *you* have a clear view to the rear of the car. Temporary mirrors can be bought for around £5, which attach via a suction cup. Position one as close to the left of the main rear view mirror as possible, so that you, as well as the learner, can see behind the vehicle.

Basic control of the driver

Learners naturally progress through three clear stages which I will refer to as First Steps, Gaining Confidence and Ready for the Test. In the 'First Steps' phase, they will require a great deal of instruction – you may have to tell them exactly what to do. When they are 'Gaining Confidence' you should only need to give them gentle hints or prompts to remind them what they should do. As they get 'Ready for the Test' they will require very little help, but may still make some mistakes. Of course, as they learn different topics at different times, you should expect them to be at different stages of learning in various topics or skills at the same time – they may be Ready for the Test for moving off and junctions and Gaining Confidence at roundabouts and dual carriageways, but only taking their First Steps at meeting traffic and driving in the rain. You will need to be aware of their various levels of accomplishment when planning where you intend to take them. Their instructor should give them a logbook showing their progress in the various skills.

Remember that any learner will learn best in a calm and positive atmosphere. Always praise their achievements and if you must be negative about one aspect of their driving, always surround the negative by two positives: 'That was a good speed when you met that traffic, but you needed to move further over to your side to give the parked car some more room. I liked the way you checked your left mirror before pulling back in.' Remember any criticism must be constructive rather than destructive, for example 'You need to move further out when passing parked cars,' rather than 'You were too close to that parked car!'

As the supervisor, you must anticipate the situation in the road ahead much earlier than normal, so that you have time to act early and prevent danger developing. Your first means of control is to tell the learner what to do, and you must also allow time for them to respond to your instructions. Ideally, you should read the road ahead so early that you have time to ask the learner what they intend to do, rather than tell them. If they answer wrongly, then you should give clear instructions.

Make sure that you give route directions clearly. It helps if you prepare the learner for the instruction by giving them a location first – 'When we get to the next junction…', followed by the instruction '…would you turn right, please.' If necessary, follow this by clarification – 'That's the road signposted for the hospital.' Avoid last moment directions or hurried instructions such as 'Turn right here.'

TIP

If you need to give more complex instructions, consider stopping first, as it is very difficult for the learner to listen to complicated instructions at the same time as trying to drive.

Many people comment that I must have the patience of a saint to be an ADI. I always reply that I don't need patience – just dual controls. It is the feeling of a total lack of control that usually prevents parents or friends of learner drivers from spending more time in the passenger seat. This can be overcome in two ways. You could wait until their instructor considers them sufficiently competent before taking them out to practise, or you could learn a few simple techniques which allow you to maintain reasonable control from the passenger seat.

Stopping the car

The only way you can have any direct control over the speed of the car is through the use of the handbrake. This is only going to be of any use at low speeds. You will be able to prevent the learner from moving off by pulling the handbrake on as hard as you can before they get too much speed up. This may stall the engine or at least slow them down sufficiently to avoid a dangerous situation. However, at higher speeds (anything over about 15mph) there is a real danger that pulling the handbrake on so hard could snap the cable. The only way to stop the car at higher speeds is to get the learner to brake.

The very first thing you should do on your first run out with them is to establish the emergency stop routine, which is detailed in Chapter 6. You should never take a learner onto public roads before they have covered this topic with their instructor. You may wish to ask their instructor to specifically cover the emergency stop for this very purpose. Remember that you must simultaneously say 'Stop' and raise your right hand by the mirror if you want them to make an emergency stop. If you want them to stop quickly but without doing an emergency stop, you should say 'More brake' or 'Gradually squeeze down on the brake pedal', and so on. Practise stopping with varying degrees of urgency in an empty car park or on a very quiet industrial estate. Make sure you have checked your mirror before asking them to stop – they may brake too sharply and stop much more quickly than you intended.

Steering

It may be necessary for you to take control of the steering wheel at times. You should grip the wheel firmly using your right hand at the '12 o'clock' position. Learners will often respond to your intrusion by actively fighting you. Be prepared to use a considerable amount of force and tell them to let go if necessary. Sometimes the opposite may apply, and as you reach over to make a small adjustment to their position, the learner may let go of the wheel altogether.

TIP

If the learner fights you when you need to steer, drop your elbow hard into the crook of theirs. This will force them to either let go or be pulled forward into the steering wheel.

Verbal control

Remember, your main method of controlling the car is through the learner: you need to tell them clearly what to do. Your tone of voice should always be calm but assertive. Speak clearly without raising your voice, and try to use positives rather than negatives – so, 'Gently brake to slow us down a little...' rather than 'Don't go so fast!'

Try also to use adverbs before the verb so that they know how to do it before they know what to do – for example, 'Smoothly bring the clutch up to biting point' rather than 'Bring the clutch up to biting point smoothly'.

Planning

In order to be able to do all of the above you will need to plan the session thoroughly. Find out what they have done with their instructor and plan to practise one specific element or skill. Try to find a route that will allow for plenty of practice, and give room for development as they progress.

Never attempt to teach the learner a new skill. That is their instructor's role, and, no matter how confident you may feel, the learner is bound to suffer if there is even the slightest conflict between what you and the instructor have said. Your role is to enable the learner to practise what their instructor has taught them.

The power of the positive

Finally, if the learner seems to be having difficulty with a particular routine, skill or manoeuvre, leave it and ask them to talk to their instructor about it. The learner will not gain anything from repeated failure. It is important that they achieve success, no matter how small a success that may be. The human brain deals much more effectively with positives than negatives. If a learner does 20 parallel parks wrong, they will have learned how to park wrongly. Even if you have to tell them exactly what to do in order for them to park correctly, then they will learn to park correctly. As they repeat this success, their brain will be reinforcing the correct routine and you will gradually be able to give them less instruction.

The whole point of practice is to repeatedly get it right. It is this repetition that reinforces the neural pathways and forms a strong pattern in the memory, allowing the learner to repeat the process with increasing accuracy and independence. It is your role to see that the learner gets plenty of beneficial repetition under their belt. Do whatever you can to keep the sessions positive. Whenever you sense negative vibes, move on to something different where the learner can achieve positive progress.

TIP

Reference is made throughout this book to its companion volume for learner drivers, the AA *Driving Skills Manual*. The AA also publishes the official Theory Test questions and *The Highway Code*.

1 Controls and Cockpit Drill

What the learner needs to be able to do

Learners must be familiar with the car's controls: their location, use and the instructions they may be given relating to their use. They must also know how to set up the car for their use and make sure it is safe before starting to drive.

How to do it

Controls

The learner will have spent some time with their instructor investigating the controls on the car. Check out any differences between that car and the car you will practise in. Make sure the learner knows how to use every control.

For example:

- light controls – are they on the stalk or separate, and how do they work?
- indicators – are they on the left or right?
- where is the horn?
- how do the demisters work?
- does the car have fog lights, and how are they operated?

The learner must also be familiar with the instrument panel warning lights. Make sure they know what each light means, and what they should do if it lights up. If it's a diesel powered car, make sure they know where the pre-heat indicator is. If the car is fitted with a tachometer or 'rev counter', make them aware of the idling speed, maximum revs (red-line) and normal range.

Cockpit drill

The learner should be familiar with the basic 'cockpit drill':

- doors
- seat
- steering
- seatbelt
- mirrors.

Make sure they follow the routine every time they enter the car.

Doors – check all doors, bonnet and boot are properly closed.

Seat – adjust distance from pedals, height, rake and head restraint. Make sure they are not too close or too far. The driver must be able to reach all controls comfortably.

Steering – if the steering wheel is adjustable, ensure the learner can hold the top of the wheel with a slight bend at the elbow.

Seatbelt – make sure it is not twisted and, if it is adjustable, that the shoulder anchor point is just above their shoulder.

Mirrors – you will not be able to see the same view as the learner, so you will need to ask if they can see:

- main mirror: the top corners of the rear window and a bit of their head restraint
- door mirrors: a bit of the side of the car and the top of the rear wheel arch at the bottom edge of the mirror.

Ask them to wriggle in their seat and get comfortable, and then check their mirrors again. Check that they can clearly see the roof of a car behind in all three mirrors.

Don't forget to check the adjustment of your own mirror, if you are using one. Place it as close to the main rear-view mirror as you can.

Before the leaner starts the engine, they must check that the handbrake is applied and the gear lever is in neutral. Discourage them from 'waggling' the gear lever. They should push the lever gently and release, checking that it springs back to its resting position. Make sure they use the button on the handbrake, and that they always pull it up as far as they can.

Practice plan

First steps

Ask them what the sequence is for the cockpit drill. Ensure that they perform each check and adjustment properly.

Ask them what they must do before starting the engine.

Gaining confidence

Ask them to carry out the cockpit drill and then observe their procedure. Correct any mistakes or out of sequence errors. If driving in poor light, ask if they might need lights.

Ready for the test

Don't prompt them at all, just watch to see that they make all checks and adjustments.

2 Moving Off and Stopping Normally

What the learner needs to be able to do

They must be able to move away safely, under full control and take up the proper position in the road. They must also be able to select and stop in a safe position, close and parallel to the kerb.

How to do it

Moving off

Having carried out the cockpit drill, the learner should check the handbrake is fully applied and the gear lever is in neutral, before starting the engine.

The routine for moving off is POM: Preparation–Observation–Manoeuvre.

Preparation

- Press the clutch fully down.
- Select first gear.
- Set the gas (gently press down on the accelerator pedal) – the engine should be set to about twice the tick-over speed.
- Find biting point – bring the clutch up smoothly until the nose of the car rises slightly and the revs drop.
- Keep feet still – the most important part.

Observation

Look all around the car from left shoulder to right shoulder, checking every window and mirror in turn. Make sure they finish by checking completely over their right shoulder into the right blind spot. You should also make these checks yourself, especially the right blind spot check, as in the early stages they may miss something approaching.

Manoeuvre

If it is not safe to move off, tell them to press the clutch back down and ease off the gas while they wait (holding bite for too long may damage the clutch). As the approaching vehicle passes, ask them to look and see if there is going to be a safe gap. If they think there will be a gap, ask them to repeat the preparation and observation phases. When it is safe, they can complete the manoeuvre:

- Release the handbrake.
- Keep feet still – this is the key to moving off smoothly. They must keep both feet absolutely still for about half a second, or until the car has moved about half a car length. If the car does not move, they have not reached biting point: instruct them to bring the clutch pedal up 1mm at a time until the car starts to move, then keep their feet still.
- As the car starts to move you will feel the engine 'smooth out'. At

this point they should 'pedal', or gently accelerate while bringing the clutch the rest of the way up.

TIP

This pedalling motion feels odd to a beginner, as their feet have to move in opposite directions. Their feet may move in the same direction, coming off the gas as the clutch comes up (more usual for right-handers) or pressing the clutch down as the gas pedal goes down (more common with left-handers). Practise this movement of the feet with the engine off to help them get the knack.

Be patient with stalling; everybody does it and beginners are likely to stall quite frequently at first. Stalling is usually due to insufficient gas or bringing the clutch up too soon or too quickly. A simple reminder to 'Keep your feet still' as they release the handbrake will usually prevent stalling.

Normal road position

They should take up a position about 1m from the kerb, if the road is wide enough. Make sure they steer accurately. At first they may need help in judging their position. If necessary, you steer to the correct position and ask them to note the position of the kerb on the windscreen wipers before letting them take over. Encourage them to look as far ahead as possible – small changes of direction become more obvious when they look further ahead. Make sure they keep a steady but slow speed at first.

Stopping

This manoeuvre uses the most important routine they will learn – Mirrors–Signal–Manoeuvre/Position –Speed–Look, or MSM/PSL.You should be very familiar with the routine yourself and probably use it automatically. For them it will be very new, and they may forget the sequence or order. You must reinforce the use of the routine from the very start. At first you should give them a stopping place to aim for, such as alongside a lamppost or by a drain cover. As they improve their skills, you could ask them to suggest an appropriate place to stop. Make sure they choose a Safe, Convenient And Legal Place (SCALP) to stop.

Mirrors – they must check the main and left mirrors for following traffic or cyclists. If they can see that the road is clear and there is no-one there to benefit from a signal, then it is all right to stop without signalling first (in fact, examiners will mark a fault if they do signal in such circumstances). If there is anyone to see it, however, they must...

Signal – left, to show they intend to pull over and park on the left.

Position – start to steer gently towards the kerb, and at the same time…

Speed – ease off the gas and gently brake.

Look – they should use the left door mirror to check their position as they slow down. You may need to help with the steering at first while they concentrate on their feet. They should stop with the left wheels 10–20cm from the kerb.

One car length from the target position, they should press the clutch pedal fully down, letting the car roll gently to a stop. Beginners may work their feet in tandem, braking even harder as the clutch pedal goes down. Again, practise with the engine off if this is a problem.

As soon as they have stopped they must apply the handbrake fully, and only then select neutral. Remind them to keep their feet on the pedals as they stop, or they may take both feet off before securing the vehicle, causing the car to lurch forward.

Practice plan

First steps

Find a long straight section of road or an empty car park to practise on.

With the engine off, let them practise bringing the clutch up smoothly in the time it takes to say 'Smoothly bring the clutch up'. With the engine on, let them practise setting the gas to the right level. Encourage them to listen to the engine.

Next, get them to practise finding biting point. Don't let them hold it for too long, and make sure they return to neutral and take both feet off the pedals between tries.

Finally, let them practise moving away and stopping normally. If the first few attempts are jerky or they keep stalling, try running through the routine with the engine off, imagining the foot positions. Remind them to make full observations before moving off.

Gaining confidence

Get them to practise moving off on a quiet road. Concentrate on timing, so that they are ready to release the handbrake as soon as it is safe. Don't let them hold biting point for more than a few seconds. When they are moving, ask them to concentrate on their road position and steering.

Practise stopping as close to a given location as possible, and the correct distance from the kerb. Make sure they stop with the steering wheel straight.

Ready for the test

They should now be ready to practise moving off and stopping normally in busy traffic. Make sure they always use the MSM/PSL routine properly, and encourage them to stop as smoothly as possible.

TROUBLESHOOTING: MOVING OFF AND STOPPING

Symptom	Cause	Remedy
MOVING OFF		
Stalling	Not enough gas	Make sure they set the revs high enough, double the tick-over speed.
	Biting point point too high	Remind them to 'smoothly bring the clutch up' – they should just feel the nose rise.
	Not keeping feet still for a moment	As the handbrake is released say 'Keep your feet still.'
Kangarooing	Not keeping feet still for a moment	As the handbrake is released say 'Keep your feet still.'
Engine Racing	Gas set too high	Make sure the gas is set correctly, double the tick-over speed.
	Clutch not at biting point	Remind them to 'smoothly bring the clutch up' – they should just feel the nose rise.
OBSERVATIONS		
Pulling out with vehicles approaching	Not making adequate observations	Remind them of the POM routine. Talk them through it once or twice, then ask them to talk themselves through it. Prompt them by asking 'Is it safe?' Observations must be left to right shoulder, finishing with a right blind spot check.
Not checking mirrors before stopping	Not using MSM/PSL routine	Remind them of to use the MSM/PSL routine, before making any change of speed or direction. Talk them through the routine, then ask them to talk themselves through. Prompt them by asking 'Is it safe to stop? Do you need give a signal?'
STOPPING NORMALLY		
Stalling	Not pushing clutch down soon enough	Clutch should go down one car length before stopping. Try saying 'Brake…brake…brake…clutch' as they stop.
Coasting	Declutching too soon	As for stalling above.
Rolling	Not applying the handbrake	Remind them of the routine for securing the vehicle: handbrake, neutral, cancel signal.
	Not keeping foot on the brake	They must keep their foot on the brake until they are completely stationary and have applied the handbrake.
Too far from/ close to kerb	Not steering accurately	Make sure they steer very gently towards the kerb and use the left door mirror to judge their position.
Not parallel to the kerb	Not straightening at the right time	Make sure that they get parallel to the kerb before straightening the steering wheel. Use markers on front and back windscreens to judge when the car is straight: park the car on a straight road, ask them to note the exact position of the kerb at the bottom of front and rear windscreens and in the left door mirror.

3 Clutch Control and Changing Gear

What the learner needs to be able to do

They need to be able to use the clutch to control the speed of the car when moving at very slow speeds, for example when manoeuvring or in slow queues of traffic. They must also use the correct gear for the speed they are travelling, changing gear smoothly and without looking down or steering erratically.

How to do it

Full details can be found in the AA *Driving Skills Manual*, but a summary of the necessary skills is given below.

Clutch control

They should prepare the car to move as in Chapter 2, but when finding biting point, they should try to keep the clutch still as soon as the revs start to drop. As they release the handbrake the car should move forward slowly.

They should immediately dip the clutch slightly by pressing down one or two millimetres on the clutch pedal. As the car slows – but before it stops – they should bring the clutch pedal back up one or two millimetres to biting point and continue to 'feather' the clutch to keep the car moving as slowly as possible. Throughout the procedure, their right foot should stay still on the gas, keeping the engine running at a steady hum. They should keep their left heel on the floor, using their ankle to operate the clutch in exactly the same way as they operate the gas pedal.

Changing gear

They should be changing up through the gears appropriately. Try to make sure that they time gear changes to take place while they are going in a straight line. This may not always be possible, but they should not be turning the steering wheel as they change gear: when changing gear on a bend or roundabout, they should steer to the required amount first, and change gear while they hold the steering wheel still with their right hand.

Sequence for changing gear

- left hand down to gear lever
- palm flat – they should not grip the gear lever
- off gas
- clutch down
- select new gear
- 'Smoothly bring the clutch up' in the time it take to say the phrase
- accelerate smoothly
- left hand back to steering wheel and left foot to resting position.

They must not look down at the gear lever, but keep their eyes on the road ahead. They should steer accurately.

The sequence is exactly the same when changing down except, of course, for the acceleration phase. They should always brake to the speed they want first, and only then change gear. They should never normally be braking and changing gear at the same time.

TIP

Note that they will have been taught that first gear should only be used when their speed is at or below walking speed. If the car is still moving, second will do.

Block changes

Not only are block changes down the gears now the norm (for example from fourth to second), but examiners will expect them to be used. The reasoning is that sequential changes – that is, changing down through all gears in turn – forces the driver to spend much more time with one hand off the steering wheel and the clutch down, and therefore not in full control of the car. Modern brakes no longer require the help that sequential gear changes give.

Practice plan

First steps

With the engine off, allow them to practise changing through the gears without looking down. Encourage them to say the sequence out loud as they practise.

On a long, straight section of quiet road, practise moving off and accelerating to 25–30mph before braking to 10mph. As their speed changes they should work their way through the gears, selecting second at 10mph.

Also practise clutch control, keeping the car moving as slowly as possible.

Gaining confidence

Practise clutch control in queuing traffic. Encourage them to keep a good gap in front, so that they can keep moving rather than stop-start driving.

Under normal driving conditions they should practise working their way through the gears, using fifth when appropriate. Remember to check that they use block changes when changing down, and only change gear when they have reached the speed they want.

Ready for the test

Make sure they are always in the appropriate gear for the speed they are doing and the road and traffic conditions. Encourage them to use lower gears for engine braking on downhill sections or when they need more power, and higher gears for fuel economy and smoothness.Make sure they can change gear smoothly on steep hills, and that they anticipate the need to change down before starting an uphill stretch.

TROUBLESHOOTING: CLUTCH CONTROL AND CHANGING GEAR

Symptom	Cause	Remedy
CLUTCH CONTROL		
Stalling	Not enough gas	Make sure they set the revs high enough, double the tick-over speed.
	Biting point too high	Make sure their foot stops just as the bonnet starts to rise and the revs drop slightly.
	Letting the revs drop too much	Make sure they keep their foot still on the gas pedal throughout the manoeuvre.
Continual stopping	Dipping the clutch too far	The clutch should only go down one or two millimetres, not all the way to the floor. Use phrases such as 'dip the clutch' and 'the thickness of a pound coin.'
CHANGING GEAR		
Mis-selecting	Gripping the gear lever	They should keep their hand flat and use the lever as gently as possible.
	Not pushing against the spring	Watch as they move the gear lever. Check that they push gently in the right direction – they may forget to push against the spring and select third instead of fifth, or they may push too hard and select first instead of third, etc.
	Clutch not down	Make sure they have the clutch pedal fully down.
	Unsure of positions	Practise with the engine off, making sure that they don't look down at the lever. If necessary, block their view.
Engine racing	Not releasing gas pedal before declutching	Make sure that they follow the sequence: off gas, clutch down…etc.
	Onto gas before clutch is fully up	Make sure that they follow the sequence: select gear, bring the clutch up smoothly, on gas… etc.
	Selected too low a gear	Make sure they select the appropriate gear. Watch carefully when they change from second to third (they may select first) or fifth to fourth (they may select second).
No acceleration	Selected too high a gear	As above.
Brake/gear overlap	Changing gear while they are still braking	They must slow down to the speed they want before changing gear. Try saying 'Brake… brake… brake… clutch' as they slow down.
Coasting	Not bringing clutch back up as soon as they have selected the new gear	As they select the new gear, remind them by saying 'Remember to bring the clutch up smoothly.'

4 Turning Left and Right

What the learner needs to be able to do

They must be able to turn from a major road into a minor road safely and under full control. They will need to use the MSM/PSL routine to ensure that other road users understand their intentions and that they corner at a suitable speed using the correct gear.

How to do it

They should use the MSM/PSL routine to guide them through the manoeuvre. They should start the routine as soon as they see a sign for the junction or the junction itself. Encourage them to look ahead for gaps between houses or parked cars to show where the side road might be.

Mirrors – they must check the main mirror and the door mirror in the direction they intend to turn.

Signal – if it is safe, they should indicate to show other road users that they intend to turn, delaying their indicators if necessary and using their brake lights to show that they are slowing down.

Position – if they intend to turn right they should move as close to the centre line as possible or into the right hand lane if there is one. If they intend to turn left, they should keep to the normal road position, 1m from the kerb.

Speed – they should slow down to take the turn safely. For a left turn they should judge their speed on what they can see around the corner. For right turns they will probably need to slow down more. As a general rule they should slow down to a fast walking speed for right turns, about 5–6mph, and always be prepared to stop.

When they have reached the desired speed they should still be about two car lengths from the turn. They must then select the appropriate gear for their speed.

If they have to stop and wait, they should stop at the turning point – when the front wheels are level with the centre line of the road into which they intend to turn.

TIP

Make sure they stop with the wheels straight. That way, a vehicle running into the back of them will push them into an empty space rather than into oncoming traffic.

Look – if they are turning right, they will need to find a safe gap in the oncoming traffic.

They now need to look into the road they intend to take, checking for obstructions which may prevent them from turning. They also need to check their door mirror to be sure no one is attempting to pass. If turning right, someone could be about to overtake, or, if turning left, a cyclist may be about to pass on their left, especially if the traffic is moving slowly.

Make sure they steer accurately, neither cutting the corner nor 'swan-necking' – swinging too wide then having to steer back to get to the correct road position.

TIP

When making any turn, remember the 'four Ss': they must not make anyone else Stop, Slow, Steer or Swear.

Practice plan

First steps

Practise judging a safe gap for turning right in traffic. On a quiet 30mph road, time how long it takes them to turn right from stationary (probably 3–4 seconds). Now drive along the same road without turning right. Start counting as they pass the junction and see how far down the road they are after 5 or 6 seconds – a safe gap. Try to spot a marker of some sort, such as a lamppost or drain cover. The relative distance between the marker and the junction shows what a safe gap would be. Make sure they are driving at an appropriate speed.

Now that they have a way of judging a safe gap, practise taking right turns on busier roads. Make sure that they have plenty of practice at clear junctions and those where they have to stop.

Practise left turns as well, saying the MSM/PSL routine out loud as they do them.

Gaining confidence

Practise turning left and right on busier roads, including right turns with boxes or from separate right turn lanes. Find some turns with traffic lights, if possible, especially those with filter lights.

Concentrate at first on getting the speed and gear right, then shift the emphasis to positioning.

Ready for the test

Practise on very busy roads, concentrating on getting their timing right. Try to approach right turns at such a speed that they do not have to stop completely.

Include junctions with lanes, yellow box markings, filter arrows, roads at acute angles (very sharp turns, almost doubling back on yourself) and Y-junctions.

TROUBLESHOOTING: TURNING LEFT AND RIGHT

Symptom	Cause	Remedy
Approaching too fast	Not spotting side road early enough	Encourage them to look further ahead. Get them to look for road signs, gaps in between houses or parked cars, street lights off to the side, etc.
	Not starting MSM/ PSL early enough	They may delay starting the routine. Say the routine aloud as soon as you can see the junction.
	Not braking sufficiently	Say 'a little more brake' until they are decelerating at the correct rate. Make sure they brake progressively, squeezing the pedal down gently.
	Releasing brake too soon	Make sure they know what speed they should be aiming for by asking 'How fast should we be going to take this corner safely?'
	Coasting	Most turns involve running down the camber of the road. If they coast around the corner, they will speed up as they turn. When they change gear make sure they bring the clutch up straight away by saying 'Bring the clutch up smoothly.'
Approaching too slowly	Over-braking	Encourage them to be gentle with the pedals. Always say 'gently brake' or 'firmly brake', so they know how much pressure to apply before they touch the brake. You can always ask for more. They may hold onto the brake for too long. When they reach the desired speed say 'off brake – that's slow enough'.
	Starting MSM/PSL too soon	Don't give the instruction to turn too soon before the junction – they may start the routine immediately rather than waiting to see the signs or road itself.
Faults in MSM/PSL	Not using the routine	Prompt them by starting to say the routine aloud or by asking 'When should you start the MSM routine?' For lapses in the individual phases, prompt them with a question, e.g. 'Is there anything behind us?', 'Do you need to signal?', 'Where should you position the car?', 'How fast do we want to be going?' or 'Are there any cyclists on your left?'
Not taking ample gaps	Misjudging the size of the gap	Remind them to look for gaps, not cars. Ask if they can see a big enough gap coming.
Cutting across oncoming traffic	Misjudging the size of the gap	As above.
Cutting corners	Turning too soon or too sharply	Remind them by saying 'Watch the policeman's toes' just before they turn.

5 Emerging Left and Right

What the learner needs to be able to do

They must be able to emerge at a T-junction safely and with due regard for other road users. They need to know how to assess the junctions as 'open' or 'closed' and how to apply the MSM/PSL routine in each case. They must also know the meanings of the road markings and signs, especially the difference between 'Stop' and 'Give Way'.

How to do it

The application of the MSM/PSL routine at T-junctions depends on the degree of visibility at the junctions. As they approach they must assess whether the junction is 'open' – that is, they can see clearly that it is safe to emerge without stopping, or 'closed' – they are unable to see clearly in either one or both directions. For both types of junction the routine starts as soon as they can see the junction itself or they can read the Stop or Give Way sign.

Mirrors – check main mirror (is anything too close behind?) and door mirror in the direction they intend to turn (is anything trying to pass on that side?).

Signal – make sure any signal given is not too early – there may be another side road before they reach the main junction.

Position – if turning right they should move over to a position as close to the centre line as is safe. If turning left they must follow the contour of the kerb as they approach, staying 1m away at all times.

Speed – they must now decide whether the junction is 'open' or 'closed'.

At a closed junction they may need to stop at the line, as they cannot see if the road is clear. They will therefore need to approach at no more than walking speed – around 4mph. About two car lengths from the line they should select first gear and immediately find biting point again, so that they roll slowly to the line, able to stop easily if necessary, but equally able to get going if there is a suitable gap in the traffic.

At the line they may still be unable to see clearly and must come to a stop. Such junctions are called 'blind' junctions and are common in older residential areas or where hedges obscure the sightlines on rural roads. At a blind junction, they must stop before creeping forwards,until they

can see far enough to emerge safely – a process sometimes known as 'peep and creep'. As soon as they see anything approaching they should stop and wait for it to pass before resuming the 'peep and creep' process.

At a Stop line they must stop, even if they can see it is safe to go. Any examiner will fail them if they continue to move, no matter how slowly.

At an 'open' junction they must slow to a speed at which they are able to safely negotiate the turn – rarely more than 10mph. They will need to select second gear about two car lengths from the line.

Look – the minimum observations at any T-junction must be Right, Left and Right again. Of course, if they must wait for passing traffic they should continue to alternate between right and left. Remind them to look for gaps, not cars. They must only cross the line when they are 100% certain that it is safe. As they turn they must look in the direction they are going.

Dual carriageways

When turning right across a dual carriageway, they must assess whether the central reservation is deep enough for their vehicle to fit fully within the space. No part of the vehicle must overhang the carriageway when stationary. If it is deep enough, they should treat the dual carriageway as two separate roads, crossing the nearest carriageway first and then waiting, if necessary, in the central reservation until it is safe to continue. If the central reservation is not deep enough, they must wait until it is safe to cross both carriageways in one go.

Remember: they must never cause any other road user to Stop, Slow, Steer or Swear.

Practice plan

First steps

Start on quiet roads, emerging to the left at closed junctions. When they are reasonably confident and have mastered the speed phase of MSM/PSL, move on to turning right.

Gaining confidence

Practise on busier roads including both open and closed junctions and a mixture of Stop and Give Way junctions.

Ready for the test

Practise emerging at all types of junctions, including crossing dual carriageways. They should aim to keep moving at Give Way lines if at all possible. Make sure that they approach at a suitable speed and select the correct gear. Their observations must be thorough and follow a routine, never taking any risks.

TROUBLESHOOTING: EMERGING LEFT AND RIGHT

Symptom	Cause	Remedy
Signalling too soon	Not scanning the side of the road on the approach	If you see their finger move towards the indicator stalk too soon, ask 'Is it safe to signal yet?'
Approaching too fast	Not starting MSM/PSL soon enough	They must spot the signs and clues earlier. Point out buildings, hedges, lampposts or kerbs opposite. Say 'Look at the sign' as soon as it is visible. If they haven't checked their mirrors by the time you can read the sign, say 'Mirrors, Signal, Manoeuvre / Position, Speed, Look' out loud.
	Not assessing 'open' or 'closed' accurately	Prompt them as you approach by asking 'Is this one open or closed?' or 'Can you see if it is safe to go?'
	Not braking firmly enough	Encourage progressive braking by saying 'Squeeze the brake pedal'. Remind them of their target speed by saying 'down to walking speed'.
Stopping unnecessarily	Not releasing the brake at the target appropriate speed	Remind them to 'try to keep moving if possible'.
	Leaving gear change too late	If their left hand is not ready by the time they are three car lengths from the line, ask 'What gear will you need?'
	Misjudging the length of traffic gaps	As they stop, start counting in seconds until the next car passes in front of you. If appropriate, say 'That gap was big enough, so look for a similar gap now.'
Incorrect road position	Not following the kerb when turning left	Usually a symptom of a fast approach. Make sure the speed is slow enough for them to have time to look at the kerb as they near the line. Remind them to stay 1m from the kerb as they are braking.
	Not looking left	Make sure they look both ways. Ask 'Are you still one metre from the kerb?'
	Incorrectly positioned when turning right	Remind them to 'stay as close to the centre line as is safe'.
Pulling out in front of other vehicles	Inadequate observations	Make sure they look at least Right, Left and Right again. Issue the 'Stop' command if necessary, then explain why. Remind them to look particularly carefully for cyclists or motorbikes.
	Misjudging the gap	Ask 'Is it safe?' or 'Can you see a safe gap?' Where possible, be specific, e.g. 'Is there enough of a gap after the red BMW?'
Not obeying Stop signs or lines	Not reading or spotting the sign	Ask 'What's special about this junction?' or 'What does the sign say?' or even 'What does a solid white line mean?'

6 Emergency Stop

What the learner needs to be able to do

They must be able to stop the car as quickly as possible under full control, as if in an emergency. Imagine a child has run out in front of them.

How to do it

Full details of the procedure and an explanation of the reasons for doing it that way may be found in the AA *Driving Skills Manual*. The procedure can be summarised as:

- No mirror checks.
- Steer straight and keep a firm grip on the wheel.
- Brake quickly, firmly and progressively. Clutch down at the last moment.
- Handbrake and neutral as soon as they stop.
- All-round observations, double-check both blind spots before driving away.

They should also be aware of the appropriate action to take in the event of a skid. Make sure they know whether your car has ABS or not.

When to do it

They will have learned a little about planning and awareness and the many factors that could affect their ability to stop effectively. Try to reinforce their understanding by highlighting these skills during normal driving. For example, when passing a school warning sign ask if it is relevant at that time of day; or in residential areas, ask them what hazards they might expect. Point out changes in road surface or weather conditions. Make sure they are always driving slowly enough to stop comfortably within the distance they can see to be safe.

You must always ask the learner to pull over and park on the left before you give them the instructions.

TIP

Try to avoid using the word 'stop' except for this particular exercise.

You should explain that you want them to do an emergency stop when you give the signal and that you will make sure it is safe first.

Safety first

Before practising this exercise you must make especially sure that you have a clear view to the rear. Your mirror (if you have one) will not give an adequate view for practising emergency stops. You will need to look all around the car yourself before giving the instruction. Ensure the road is clear both behind and ahead. Choose a section of road where you will be clearly visible for 100m in either direction. Look into any side roads you pass to check for vehicles that may be pulling out and following you.

The signal for the emergency stop is to raise your right hand level with the rear-view mirror and at the same time say clearly 'Stop!'

Practice plan

First steps

Choose a very quiet, straight road to practise the routine at about 15mph without actually braking hard. The learner should be concentrating on the sequence of actions.

Gaining confidence

Gradually increase the speed and encourage them to brake harder. The exercise is easier at higher speeds.

Ready for the test

Practise on different road surfaces and in all weather conditions if possible. On wider roads you may be able to stop from higher speeds, but make sure you allow much more room for other traffic.

TROUBLESHOOTING: EMERGENCY STOP

Symptom	Cause	Remedy
Slow reactions	Shock	Make sure they are prepared, and avoid raising your voice. Warn them again a few seconds before giving the instruction.
	Otherwise engaged	In the early stages make sure they are settled at a steady speed and not doing anything else. In the later practice stages, deliberately wait until they are changing gear. Explain that the stop takes priority over anything else.
	Naturally slower reactions	There are many electronic games and toys that may help develop quicker reactions (such as Boppit).
Not stopping quickly	Not braking progressively	Encourage them to squeeze the pedal down firmly as they brake.
	Coasting (clutch down too soon)	Reinforce the need to de-clutch only at the last moment. Practise at slower speed and without braking hard, until they are de-clutching as late as possible.
ABS operating or skidding	Coasting	ABS often operates only when the clutch is depressed. Reinforce the need to de-clutch only at the last moment.
	Braking too hard	Check they are not stamping on the brake. Remind them to squeeze the pedal. Make sure they keep their heel on the floor and swivel their foot from gas to brake. Watch their right thigh if you cannot see their foot.
Stalling	Not de-clutching before stopping	Remind them that they need to de-clutch before stopping. As they slow say 'Brake, brake, brake… clutch.'
Handbrake/ neutral before stopping	Rushing	Remind them that they must stop completely before securing the vehicle.
Not coming to a full halt	Releasing footbrake before stopped	Remind them to keep the footbrake on until the car is stationary.
	Releasing footbrake before handbrake is applied (rolling)	Remind them to keep their feet still until the vehicle is secured.
Poor observations before moving off	Forgetting all observations	Remind them that they are in the middle of the road; they must look all around and check both blind spots.

7 MSM/PSL – Hazard Routine

What the learner needs to be able to do

The Mirrors–Signal–Manoeuvre/Position–Speed–Look routine (often shortened to MSM/PSL) is fundamental to learning to drive. They must use it before making any change of speed or direction. It is also called the 'hazard routine' – it must be used whenever they see a hazard.

How to do it

The learner must be familiar with the following definitions:

- A *manoeuvre* is any change of speed or direction.
- A *hazard* is anything that may cause you to manoeuvre – that is, to change your speed or direction.

The important word here is 'may'. They might be able to negotiate some hazards without actually having to change speed or direction at all, but the potential danger is there, so they must always be prepared in case the situation changes suddenly.

'Mirrors–Signal–Manoeuvre' reminds them to check their mirrors and give a signal before they make any change of speed or direction. By definition, they will use the routine every time they spot a hazard.

Mirrors

As soon as you see any hazard, watch the learner's eyes. They should check their main mirror and then the door mirror in the direction they may need to go. It is essential that these mirror checks become second nature, so you must reinforce them at every opportunity. Be especially careful that the learner does not do anything else until the mirrors have been checked.

Signal

Having checked the mirrors, the learner then needs to decide whether it is necessary to signal.

TIP

As a general rule they should give a signal if it would be of benefit to any other road user. If there is no-one there to see the signal, then it is not necessary to give one.

It is important that the learner understands and uses the full range of signals. For example, they should not normally indicate right to pass a stationary vehicle. In this case the signal will be their road position: pulling out early enables a following car to see the obstruction and know that you are going to go around it.

TIP

This may go against the grain with older drivers who were taught that they must indicate, but it is now the accepted practice. In fact, it is now considered to be bad practice to signal right when overtaking parked cars, as the signal could mislead others into thinking that you are going to turn right – where there are parked cars, there are often more junctions too.

The timing of signals must be accurate. Make sure that the learner does not give misleading signals by indicating too early or late.

Manoeuvre

The third part of MSM, the manoeuvre itself, is divided into three more phases: Position–Speed–Look, or PSL.

Position

The learner should then take up the proper position in the road. Unless they are turning right, this should be about 1m from the kerb (on narrow roads stay centrally between the kerb and the centre of the road). If there are marked lanes, they should stay centrally in their lane. If they are turning right, then they should position themselves to the right of their lane, or as close to the centre line as is safe. Do not allow them to swing out in the opposite direction before turning: having signalled they must take up the correct position and maintain it until they execute the turn.

Speed

They must brake to the speed that they want and only then change into the appropriate gear for that speed. Discourage them from braking and changing gear at the same time.

If there is any question about what speed they may require, for example, when approaching a traffic light that has been on red for as long as it has been visible (it could change to green), then they should delay the gear change until they are certain of their actions. In the case of the traffic light, they should wait until they are sure that they will have to stop or have slowed to walking speed, before changing into first gear. If the light changes to green before they reach this point, then they can change directly into second gear.

TIP

Remember that block changes are now the norm (see Chapter 3).

Look

Just before starting to steer, they should look in the door mirror in the direction they intend to steer or into the blind spot on that side. They must also look where they intend to go. If turning left or right, they need to be certain that there are no pedestrians about to cross as they turn.

TIP

A large part of the following chapters is concerned with the application of the MSM/PSL routine for specific circumstances. It is vital that they get used to using the routine as soon as possible.

Practice plan

First steps

Get them to practise judging distances (in metres) in your local area, for example from the front door to the house opposite; from the drive to the end of the road; the distance between the lampposts.

They should practise the MSM hazard routine by talking aloud through the routine on quiet roads. Ask them to concentrate on the major hazards only – those that will definitely make them change speed or direction. For example, to overtake a parked vehicle they might say 'Parked car on my side. Checking main and right mirrors – all clear. Signal not needed. Position out to pass one metre away. Speed a little slower for the narrower gap. Looking in my left mirror to check I'm past and pulling back in.' If they have problems giving such a commentary, ask them to give a commentary as you drive for a few minutes.

Gaining confidence

As they become more proficient, try to include the minor hazards as well – those that might make them change speed or direction. You may find that they never manage to complete the whole sequence. If there are so many hazards that they only ever manage to say 'Mirrors, signal…mirrors, signal' then they need to slow down.

Practise in busier areas where there are more major hazards. As well as reciting the routine, ask them to say what could happen with minor hazards, for example:

'Dog on left, off the lead – could run across road so Mirrors – car close behind so Signal with brake lights. Position – move further from kerb and Speed – slowing in case. Looking that I'm safely past.'

Ready for the test

By now they should be at ease with reciting the routine aloud. Ask them to run fully through the sequence for every hazard. They should be able to prioritise the various hazards and be prepared to respond to any that develop. Get them to practice spotting the hazards as soon as they can: a game of who can spot the hazards first, them or you, can help develop their perception. Encourage them to scan as far ahead as possible so that they have time to run the full sequence.

8 Dealing with Traffic

What the learner needs to be able to do

They need to be able to deal with situations involving other road users, including meeting traffic, crossing traffic, overtaking and queuing.

How to do it

Meeting traffic

A meeting situation is one where an obstruction has narrowed the road so much that only one vehicle may pass at a time. The learner driver must understand the rule of priority: if your side of the road is blocked you must give priority to oncoming traffic. The same rule applies in reverse: if your side of the road is clear, you have priority over oncoming traffic. However, you must never assume that the other vehicle is going to let you through first.

When assessing the gap they should consider the speed, position and size of the oncoming vehicle. Encourage them to be considerate towards drivers of large vehicles for whom stopping is more difficult. The learner may choose to give way, even when they have priority, but must take into account any following traffic.

As always, MSM/PSL is the guide to handling meeting situations.

Mirrors – as soon as they can see the obstruction, no matter which side it is on, they must check their main mirror (following traffic) and the right door mirror if they need to pull out. They must then decide who has priority. If they must give way they should...

Signal – by positioning their vehicle to get a clear view, but allowing ample room for the oncoming vehicle to pass easily. The learner should avoid using the right indicator unless they need to stop and their position makes it look to following traffic as if they have parked. Signalling in any other situation could be interpreted as an intent to force their way through.

Position – if they must stop, they should 'hold back' about two car lengths from the obstruction and far enough out so that they get a clear view of the road ahead without obstructing oncoming traffic.

Speed – ideally, the learner should slow down enough that the oncoming vehicle has time to pass through the gap before you come to a stop.

Look – they should continue to look past the obstruction for a safe gap and use mirrors to check that following traffic is not attempting to overtake.

When passing through the gap they must take care to leave enough room – a parked car's door could swing open, or a builder's skip may hide workers from view. If the gap is so restricted that they must pass closer than 1m, then they must proceed slowly enough to stop – no more than 15mph.

If the obstruction is on the other side of the road, MSM/PSL is still used. In this case they must be prepared to stop if an oncoming vehicle forces its way through. They must reduce their speed as they approach, but should avoid unintentionally signalling that they are giving way by slowing too much and pulling closer to the kerb. They must try to use their speed and position to make it clear that they intend to take priority, but must also ensure that they are able to stop safely if necessary.

Crossing traffic

Nearly every right turn involves crossing the path of other traffic. The learner must be able to judge a safe gap and be prepared to take the first suitable gap that arises. As a pedestrian they should be able to judge a safe gap to walk across the road; a similar sized gap should be ample for them to drive across. Make sure they are cautious of speeding traffic or higher speed limits.

Help them to anticipate gaps by watching for signals given by other road users. They must never act on a signal alone, but should wait to see it confirmed by a change of speed or direction.

When crossing dual carriageways they must assess the depth of the central reservation. If it is deep enough, they may cross the first carriageway and wait in the central reservation for a suitable gap to complete the manoeuvre. If the central reservation is not deep enough for them to position the vehicle completely between the lines, then they must wait for a safe gap in both directions so that they can cross in one go. They should not wait at an angle in the middle as this makes proper observations difficult, but should always stop at right angles to the line.

Overtaking

Overtaking is defined as passing another vehicle, be it stationary or moving. In this manoeuvre the MSM/PSL routine is modified slightly to include an extra PSL phase before the main MSM/PSL. This is to allow the learner to get into a position where they can see clearly whether it is safe to overtake. There will also be an extra mirror check in the MSM phases, making it Mirrors–Signal–Mirror–Manoeuvre.

They must decide first whether the overtake is necessary, safe and legal.

- Do they intend to turn off soon, or is the vehicle they intend to overtake likely to turn off? Are they travelling substantially faster than the vehicle ahead? Is there a reason why the vehicle in front is going more slowly?
- Can they see far enough ahead to see a safe gap? Are there any junctions ahead? Is the road ahead hidden by a bend, hill or dip?
- Do they have a solid white line on their side of the centre line? Would they have to exceed the speed limit in order to complete the manoeuvre?

Only if these three requirements can be satisfied and there is no risk involved should the learner consider overtaking.

TIP

Remember, on your side of the car you have a very limited view of the road ahead: don't allow the learner to proceed with an overtake unless *you* are sure it is safe.

Preparation (PSL)

They should first *position* themselves so that they have a good view of the road ahead. Keeping well back allows for a better view, especially around larger vehicles.

They should consider changing to a lower gear to get more acceleration in reserve at the *speed* they are doing.

They must *look* past the vehicle to spot any hazards which may cause it to move out. They may need to look down the inside of the vehicle ahead if the road is bending gently to the left.

Provided they, and you, are satisfied that it is safe to proceed they must then use the MSM/PSL routine:

Mirrors – check nothing is attempting to overtake your vehicle.

Signal – indicate right to show that they intend to pull out. They must give the vehicle in front time to respond to this signal if necessary. They may need to pull out themselves, so allow at least four flashes before continuing. That should be the time it takes to make one last check…

Mirror – another check in the right mirror is needed to check it is safe, and this should be confirmed by a quick blind-spot check.

Position – only when they are 100% certain it is safe, they should pull out, making sure that they have timed this so that they never get too close to the other vehicle.

Speed – they should accelerate so that they pass briskly but stay within the speed limit.

Look – they should use the main and left mirrors to check they are safely past before pulling back in. When they can see the front of the vehicle in the main mirror they are far enough past. They must not cut in or slow down immediately after overtaking. If they changed down to pass, make sure they return to the appropriate gear.

Queuing traffic

Use queues as an opportunity to practise clutch control.

- They should try to keep moving whenever possible by maintaining a good gap in front and looking well ahead in order to anticipate the movement of traffic.
- They must never get so close that they are unable to see the tyres of the vehicle in front touching the road, plus about 1m of tarmac (this is the 'Tyres and Tarmac' rule, see Chapter 17).
- They must leave entrances to side roads or premises clear so that oncoming traffic can turn in.
- They must not stop on pedestrian crossings, but should wait behind the line until there is space beyond the crossing to proceed. The same applies to other junctions, traffic lights and roundabouts: they must wait behind the Give Way line until there is somewhere to go.
- If they must stop for more than a few seconds then they should use the handbrake and take their foot off the footbrake, especially at night when the brake lights could dazzle the driver behind.
- If the queue is stationary for more than a few minutes, they should consider turning the engine off.

Practice plan

First steps

Meeting – on quiet roads, concentrate on judging the width of the gap: Is there enough room for two cars to pass? Practise slowing down and getting going again on a clear stretch of road, before repeating the exercise with parked cars but no oncoming traffic. Prompt them by saying MSM/PSL out loud.

Crossing – continue to practise turning and emerging to the right as described in Chapters 4 and 5.

Overtaking – at first they should practise on slow-moving vehicles. Make sure they leave ample space when passing, especially for cyclists or vehicles used by disabled people.

Queuing – try to find short queues for them to practise both their clutch control and keeping space around their vehicle. Town centre road-works are often a good choice as there are likely to be side roads you can use as escape routes. Encourage them to keep moving if at all possible.

Gaining confidence

Meeting – practise in residential areas where there will be plenty of parked cars and a reasonable amount of traffic. Get them to concentrate on the speed of approach, so that they keep moving whenever possible, and keeping a safe distance from the obstruction. Practise getting to the holdback position even when there is no approaching traffic.

Crossing – try to find a dual carriageway where they can practise crossing both in one go and by stopping in the middle. Get them to practise right turns in busier traffic and where there is substantial pedestrian activity.

Overtaking – practise overtaking on dual carriageways. Make sure they overtake without slowing down first if possible.

Queuing – try to include major junctions in very busy traffic as a realistic exercise in queuing skills.

Ready for the test

Meeting – practise in busy urban areas. Encourage them to keep moving, no matter how slowly, when possible.

Crossing – busy urban roads should provide ample practice in taking smaller gaps. Encourage them to get ready to move as soon as they stop, and make sure that they keep looking for signs or signals from other road users. They must always check for themselves that it is safe before acting on invitations from other road users to go first.

Overtaking – lots of practice on major rural roads will be needed in order to find an opportunity to overtake on single carriageways. Try to use wide roads with long straight stretches if possible.

Queuing – rush-hour traffic in a busy town centre should provide all the practice needed. Alternatively, try to find some major roadworks with traffic lights. Encourage them to keep moving slowly but maintain a safe gap at all times. Try to include queues on hilly terrain.

TROUBLESHOOTING: DEALING WITH TRAFFIC

Symptom	Cause	Remedy
MEETING TRAFFIC		
Going through when not safe	Misjudging the width of the gap	If there is any question whether there is enough room to pass or not, the answer is always 'No'. They must be 100% sure it is safe.
	Not understanding the rules of priority	Remind them of the rules. As soon as you see the meeting situation ahead ask them 'Who will have priority here?'
	Misreading the intentions of oncoming traffic	As soon as they see the oncoming vehicle ask them 'What do you think the driver's going to do?'
Getting too close to the obstruction	Not holding back	Usually due to a fast approach or late decision to stop. Remind them to slow down on approach and prompt to make a decision earlier by asking 'Is it safe to go through?'
	Passing too close	Ask 'What could happen as you pass this car?' Make sure they have seen any pedestrians or passengers in the car.
CROSSING TRAFFIC		
Cutting in front of oncoming vehicles	Inability to judge a safe gap	Practise right turns and emerges so that they are confident in their ability to pull away. Time how long it takes them to cross to the other side of the road. Add two seconds as a safety margin. Find out how far away from a junction that gap would place an oncoming vehicle. Spot the next furthest landmark, such as a lamppost, driveway or phone box. If it is clear up to that point, they have a safe gap.
	Moving away too slowly	Make sure they set enough gas and have a firm biting point. Avoid stalling by reminding them to keep their feet still for a moment, then 'pedal'.
Not taking ample gaps	Inability to judge a safe gap	See above.
	Lack of confidence moving away	Practise moving away. Remind them that they can ensure a quick getaway by performing a hill start on the flat.

TROUBLESHOOTING: DEALING WITH TRAFFIC

Symptom	Cause	Remedy
OVERTAKING		
Pulling out when it is not safe	Lack of adequate observations	Make sure they carry out the extra PSL to enable them to get a good view of the road ahead before starting MSM/PSL. Ask them if it is safe to overtake.
	Inadequate rear observations	Make sure they check the mirrors correctly, and remind them to make a final bind-spot check before pulling out.
Not overtaking when necessary	Lack of confidence	Encourage them by practising on dual carriageways and wide roads where visibility is good.
Passing too slowly	Use of too high a gear or too little acceleration	Remind them that they may need to change down to get more acceleration. Encourage them to press down firmly on the gas pedal.
Passing too close	Not giving adequate clearance	Remind them to pull out far enough using such prompts as 'The cyclist may wobble as we pass him,' or 'How far away should we be as we pass this car?'
QUEUING		
Stalling, engine racing or shuddering	Poor clutch control	Practise clutch control on a quiet road until they are familiar with the position of biting point. Remember, it may be completely different in their instructor's car.
Following too closely	Not looking far enough ahead	Encourage them to look further by asking them what the van/ bus/red car six vehicles ahead is doing. Remind them of the 'Tyres and Tarmac' rule as they close up.
	Closing the gap by driving too fast	Remind them to use clutch control to keep the car moving slowly. Only keep pace and maintain the gap ahead.
Dropping back too far	Not looking far enough ahead	See above.
	Not keeping the clutch at biting point	If they push the clutch fully down when stopping for a short time, it will take much longer to get going again. Remind them to anticipate the movement of traffic ahead by looking further ahead, and to make sure they are ready to move when the second car ahead moves.
Blocking side roads, entrances, junctions or crossings	Inattention to surroundings	Remind them to scan all around them, not just the situation ahead. If necessary, stop them before they start to move into such a position.

9 Pedestrian and Level Crossings

What the learner needs to be able to do

They must be able to approach and negotiate pedestrian and level crossings safely and with due regard for other road users. They must know the differences between the various crossings, and how to recognise them.

How to do it

They should have learned about the various types of crossings in their study of driving theory, and should be familiar with zebra, pelican, puffin and toucan pedestrian crossings as well as the school crossing patrol and railway level crossings. They should know that pelican, puffin and toucan are light-controlled crossings. Level crossings – where the road crosses a railway track – also fall into the light-controlled category.

Pedestrian-controlled crossings

Zebra crossings are controlled by pedestrians and require special care.

- If a pedestrian is waiting to cross, the learner should slow down and stop, if necessary, to allow them to cross.
- If a pedestrian is on the crossing, the learner must give way and allow them to cross.

The learner should look for the orange beacons on either side of the crossing and the zigzag markings running along either side of the road.

They should use the MSM/PSL routine on approach:

Mirrors – as soon as they spot the crossing they should check the main mirror, as they may need to slow down suddenly if a pedestrian steps out unexpectedly. They must do this before looking to see if there is anyone waiting to cross. They should scan both sides of the road, looking for any pedestrian who is close enough to the crossing to be able to use it.

Signal – brake lights warn any following vehicle that they are slowing down. They should also consider a slowing-down arm signal to let the pedestrian know that they are slowing; the pedestrian may then cross earlier.

Position – they should maintain a normal road position, but should be wary of pedestrians who may step into the road before the crossing.

Speed – they must slow down, even if they cannot see anyone waiting: pedestrians may step out at the very last moment.

Look – they should continue to scan the surrounding area as they near the crossing. If they do have to stop, they must wait until the pedestrians are completely off the road before proceeding.

TIP

At any type of crossing the learner should stop if required behind the stop line, and apply the handbrake.

The school crossing patrol is essentially a temporary zebra crossing and the learner should use MSM/PSL as above. If the patrol is standing at the kerb with the 'lollipop' stop sign raised, traffic must stop and allow the patrol to take up their position in the road. Of course, pedestrians are unpredictable – particularly schoolchildren – so the learner must be especially careful of those who cross without using the patrol, or some distance from the crossing point.

Light-controlled crossings

More detail is given in the AA *Driving Skills Manual*, but here we shall consider all light-controlled crossings together.

The learner should be looking far enough ahead to spot the lights in good time. As soon as they see the lights they should start the MSM/PSL routine:

Mirrors – they should check the main mirror before looking to see if any pedestrians are at or near the crossing.

Signal – only if they can see pedestrians waiting at or approaching the crossing should they need to slow down enough to stop if required – brake lights may be required.

Position – they should maintain normal road position.

Speed – they must approach at such a speed that they can comfortably stop should the crossing lights change. At puffin or toucan crossings the lights will almost certainly not change to red unless there are pedestrians waiting. For these two crossings only, it is not necessary to brake on the approach if there are no pedestrians near; easing off the gas slightly will be ample deceleration. However, at pelican crossings the lights can change even when no pedestrians are evident, so the learner must slow down sufficiently to be able to stop at an amber light if necessary. Try to prevent the learner slowing down too much if the lights are green; pedestrians may assume the lights are changing and may step out too soon.

Look – they should continue to scan the surrounding area as they approach.

If they have to stop at a pelican crossing, the learner must wait for pedestrians to clear the crossing before proceeding. They may need to be reminded that a flashing amber light means that they may go if the crossing is clear – they do not have to wait for the green light.

Level crossings

Most level crossings have barriers and are controlled by light signals. Warning signs will be evident on the approach. Signs warn of the crossing and indicate the likelihood of queuing traffic. A solid amber light is followed by flashing red lights and an audible signal. You must stop behind the white line and wait until the signals have stopped and the barriers are fully up before proceeding.

Learners should treat level crossings in exactly the same way as any other light-controlled crossing. If the crossing is clear, remind them that they may still need to slow down, as the road may be very uneven as it crosses the railway tracks.

At any type of crossing the learner must avoid stopping on the crossing itself, especially in queues. Remind them if you don't think they have sufficient room to clear the crossing.

They should also check their left mirror before moving away from a crossing: pedestrians may try to cross in their blind spot, or a cyclist could have drawn level as they waited at the crossing.

Summary

Try to encourage the learner to anticipate and plan for all types of crossings. They should be actively seeking them out whenever they are driving in an area where they are likely to be found. Look out for signs for schools and railway stations. Ask prompting questions to make them aware of the increased chance of encountering a crossing of some sort.

Practice plan

First steps

Ask the learner to identify the types of crossings as soon as they are visible. Encourage them to say the MSM/PSL routine out loud as they approach.

Gaining confidence

Try to plan routes that include as many crossings as possible. If the learner is still at school, letting them drive to or from school will give them practice dealing with crossing patrols and schoolchildren. Town centres should provide practice of other types of pedestrian crossings, while level crossing are usually found in or near villages or small towns (a road atlas will help you to locate any near you).

Ready for the test

The learner should be able to deal confidently with any type of crossing. Ask them to check with their instructor if there are any crossings on test routes that may require special practice.

TROUBLESHOOTING: PEDESTRIAN AND LEVEL CROSSINGS

Symptom	Cause	Remedy
Not checking mirrors first on approach	Not seeing crossing early enough	Encourage them to look further ahead and to scan the sides of the road as well. Make sure they see any advance warning signs by asking them 'What does that sign tell you?'
	Incorrect use of MSM/PSL	Get them to say the routine out loud.
Approaching too fast	Not identifying the type of crossing	As different types of crossings require the use of different speeds on approach, it is vital that they can identify them accurately from a distance. Get them to practise when they are a passenger.
	Not starting MSM/PSL soon enough	Encourage them to look further ahead and to scan the sides of the road as well. Make sure they see any advance warning signs by asking them 'What does that sign tell you?'
	Inadequate braking	Ask 'At what speed do we need to approach?'
	Not anticipating pedestrian movements	Point out any pedestrians who may be about to use the crossing. Check they have seen pedestrians by asking 'Is it safe?'
Approaching too slowly	Not anticipating pedestrian movements	Ask 'Does it look as if anyone wants to cross?'
Remaining stationary at flashing amber	Unsure of meaning of lights	On the approach to a pelican crossing ask 'What does a flashing amber light mean?'
Moving off before it is safe	Inadequate observations	Make sure they check it is safe before moving off.
Stopping on a crossing in a queue	Inadequate observations	Ask 'What do the zigzag lines mean?' or 'What if the lights change now?'
Not taking ample gaps	Misjudging the size of the gap	Remind them to look for gaps, not cars. Ask if they can see a big enough gap coming.
Cutting across oncoming traffic	Misjudging the size of the gap	As above.
Cutting corners	Turning too soon or too sharply	Remind them by saying 'Watch the policeman's toes' just before they turn.

10 Crossroads

What the learner needs to be able to do

They must be able to recognise, approach and negotiate crossroads safely and with due regard for other road users. They should understand the rules of priority, and the differences between marked and unmarked crossroads.

How to do it

A crossroads is the junction of a major and a minor road – traffic on the major road will pass through uninterrupted, while that on the minor road will have to stop or give way. When both roads are of similar size, or where traffic flow is often busy, the junction is likely to be controlled by traffic lights.

On the major road

Going straight ahead

The learner must be prepared for the worst possible scenario – a vehicle pulling out of the side road without seeing them. This is much more likely to occur at a crossroads than at a T-junction, as it may appear to the driver that their road simply continues ahead: road markings may be faded or difficult to see, or the signs obscured by vegetation.

Normally there will be a crossroads hazard warning sign about 100m from the junction, but this may not be easily visible. As soon as the learner notices a side road, they should check the opposite side of the road to look for a corresponding side road making the junction a crossroads. The instant they recognise that there is a crossroads ahead they should start the MSM/PSL routine:

Mirrors – they should check the main mirror to see if it would be safe to brake if necessary, giving the following car a warning by using the brake lights. They should also check the right door mirror, in case they need to pull out if a car emerges from the road on the left.

Signal – the learner could use their brake lights to show a following vehicle that they are slowing down.

Position – on narrower roads they should maintain their normal position, but on a wider road they may pull out slightly to make it easier for an emerging vehicle to see them.

Speed – they should slow down a bit in case something does emerge unexpectedly (a 5–10mph reduction is reasonable).

Look – as they approach the crossroads they should look into both side roads, right then left, to check for emerging traffic.

TIP

If a vehicle does emerge unexpectedly, they should perform an emergency stop. Their reduced speed should make this much more controlled.

Turning

Turning from the major to a minor road is essentially the same as the normal turn – see Chapter 4. The main difference is that they also need to look into the road opposite the one they are taking and be aware of any vehicle attempting to cross their path.

The one situation requiring special care is when both the learner and an oncoming vehicle both intend to turn to their respective right – that is they are going in opposite directions. The preferred option is for the two vehicles to turn offside-to-offside (driver's-side to driver's-side), so that they pass behind each other. This allows for a better view of the road they are to cross and is much safer than passing nearside-to-nearside. If the crossroads is a staggered junction and the road to the right is closer, then it is clear that to pass nearside-to-nearside would be preferable.

TIP

To avoid this problem, make sure that the learner spots the other vehicle's signal as early as possible. They can then slow down enough to let the other vehicle turn before they reach the junction themselves.

On the minor road

Emerging to the left or right at a crossroads is essentially the same as the normal emerge outlined in Chapter 5. However, the extra road opposite needs to be included in the observations, so that they become Right, Left, Ahead and Right again.

Here too the rules of priority need to be considered.

The rules of priority

Any vehicle intending to cross the path of another vehicle must give way.

- Emerging to the left: you must give way to traffic on the major road, but you have priority over a vehicle turning in the same direction from the road opposite.
- Going straight ahead: you must give way to traffic on the major road, but have priority over vehicles emerging in any direction from the road opposite.
- Emerging to the right: you must give way to traffic on the major

road and also to traffic emerging from the road opposite, except vehicles turning to their right.

This last situation requires special consideration. In this case both vehicles will be crossing each other's paths: neither has priority. Communication is needed between the two drivers to establish who is going to go first. The learner must make eye contact with the other driver. They should look for the tell-tale signs: a driver looking left and right, but avoiding direct eye contact, is almost certainly going to go first, while a driver who stops short of the give way line and looks directly at the learner, is likely to let the learner go first. The learner should keep watching for signals given by the other driver, such as a wave or flashed lights, but must never act on them without first confirming for themselves that it is safe to proceed.

Unmarked crossroads

These are usually found in housing estates or country lanes and require special care, as no-one has priority in any direction. The learner must approach these as if they were a totally blind junction, slowing right down so that they can stop if necessary where the line would be. They must make careful observation into each road and only proceed when they have determined that it is totally safe.

Light-controlled crossroads

These are generally much easier for the learner to negotiate.

- They should use the MSM/PSL routine as normal and obey the traffic light signals.
- They should look for any filter arrows that may allow them to proceed by stopping any opposing traffic.
- Learners may need reminding that green lights mean 'Go if it is safe', not 'Go'.
- They might attempt to turn right on the green light, forgetting that oncoming traffic has priority. If their light is green, they may cross the line and wait in the middle of the junction until there is a safe gap to cross, or if a filter arrow indicates that opposing traffic has been stopped and they may proceed.
- If the lights turn red while they are still in the middle of the crossroads, they should allow the last oncoming vehicle to pass and then promptly complete their turn: it is important that they clear the junction.

(For the rules regarding yellow box junctions, see Chapter 10 of the AA *Driving Skills Manual*.)

On the approach to a light-controlled junction, you might wish to remind the learner of the meaning of the different lights. Ask them what the various colours mean. You should expect the answer 'Stop' for all except green, which should be 'Go if it is safe'. Do not allow them to pass a red light under any circumstances, and make sure that they are always prepared to stop should the light turn amber. An examiner will fail any candidate who fails to stop at a red light or passes an amber light when they would have been able to stop.

Staggered crossroads

The learner should treat staggered crossroads in the same way as normal crossroads, except when going straight ahead on the minor road. In this case the degree of stagger – that is, the distance between the two minor roads – determines how the learner should signal. When going ahead at a normal crossroads, no signal is necessary, but at a staggered crossroads they should signal left and then right (or vice versa, of course) when the two roads are more than two car lengths apart.

Practice plan

First steps

Start by taking them straight ahead on the major road. Make sure they use MSM/PSL as they approach the crossroads, slowing down slightly as they get near.

Then move on to turning from the major road into the minor, taking left turns first before progressing to right turns. Remind them to make the extra observation into the road opposite, and check that they are sure about the rule of priority when turning right.

Gaining confidence

Get them to practise emerging from the minor road, first to the left and then to the right. Gradually work up from very quiet to busier areas, but avoid peak traffic periods.

Progress to busier areas for right turns off the major road paying particular attention to positioning – they should be close to the centre line and waiting, if necessary, at the turning point.

Ready for the test

Practise any staggered, light controlled and unmarked crossroads you can find. Try to include crossroads with more than one lane and those with filter arrows if possible. Make sure you practise the examiner's favourite – right turns at light controlled crossroads with no filter arrows. The learner should be able to negotiate any type of crossroads in any direction in any traffic conditions.

TROUBLESHOOTING: CROSSROADS

Symptom	Cause	Remedy
Not recognising crossroads	Poor observation	Prompt them by asking 'What type of junction are we approaching?' or 'What does that sign mean?'
Not checking mirrors	Incorrect use of MSM/PSL	Talk them through the routine a couple of times, then ask them to talk themselves through it.
Not slowing down	Incorrect use of MSM/PSL	As above. Also ask them 'What is the worst thing that could happen here?'
	Not spotting the junction	Ask 'What do you see in the road ahead?'
Not looking into road opposite as turn onto main road	Forgetting the extra observation	Remind them by saying 'Look right, left, ahead and right again', or asking 'Is it safe?'
Turning or emerging when not safe	Misunderstanding the rules of priority	Ask 'Who has priority here?' Prompt them to make proper observations by asking 'What is that driver going to do?'
	Unable to judge a safe gap	Refer to Chapter 4 or 5 as appropriate.
	Not communicating with other drivers	Ask 'What is the car opposite going to do?'
Not stopping for red or amber lights	Not slowing sufficiently on approach	As they approach the lights ask 'What could the traffic lights do?'
Not acting on filter arrows	Not noticing filter light	Make sure they see the filter light – it may only appear on the secondary lights in front of them, rather than the primary lights at the line.
Incorrect signals at staggered crossroads	Not assessing the gap between the staggered roads	Ask 'Will you have enough space to straighten out before turning into the new road?' or 'Do you need to signal here?'

Other faults relating to turning or emerging can be referred to in Chapters 4 and 5.

11 Roundabouts

What the learner needs to be able to do

They will need to show that they can negotiate roundabouts smoothly and safely. They should approach at a safe speed, in the appropriate position and indicating correctly. They should join the roundabout smoothly and with due consideration for other road users, taking the correct course around the roundabout and leaving at the appropriate exit.

How to do it

Full details of the routines can be found in the AA *Driving Skills Manual*. A summary is reproduced on the next page for quick reference. Essentially the routine for any roundabout consists of two MSM/PSL routines: the first on the approach to and joining the roundabout, and the second in preparation for leaving the roundabout.

By the time you are practising on roundabouts your learner should be very familiar with the MSM/PSL routine – encourage them to say it aloud as they use it. Not only does this reinforce the routine, but also it allows you to hear what they are thinking before they act. This should allow time for you to intervene should the need arise.

The biggest problem is usually the learner's inexperience in judging suitable gaps. Be patient. This skill takes lots of practice to acquire. You can help best by identifying a suitable gap well in advance and asking if they have seen it. Anticipation is the key here, and from your experience you will be able to anticipate gaps much earlier. Help them look where you are looking by asking, for example, 'Is the gap after the blue car big enough?'

Make sure that they are ready to move if they have stopped or, if they are still moving, that they are steering accurately and in the right gear to move away. When on the roundabout pay particular attention to their steering. Make sure that they stay in position without cutting across lanes or the course of other traffic. Be particularly aware of traffic on your left when leaving.Be prepared to take over the steering if necessary.

Practice plan

First steps

Practise slowing and changing down on a quiet, straight road as if approaching a roundabout, making sure the road behind is clear. Practise slowing to 20mph, 10mph, walking

ROUNDABOUTS: SUMMARY	First Exit	Right	Straight / Intermediate
Approaching			
Mirrors	main and left	main and right	main and left
Signal	left	right	do not indicate
Position	left or left lane	right or right lane	left lane unless busy
Speed	20mph or less	20mph or less	20mph or less
Look	RLR again	RLR again	RLR again
Leaving (at exit before)			
Mirrors	left	left and left blind spot	left and left blind spot
Signal	left still on	left	left
Position	keep left	stay in right lane	stay in lane
Speed	keep a steady speed	keep a steady speed	keep a steady speed
Look	left and ahead	left and ahead	left and ahead

speed and actually stopping briefly. Each time make sure they select the appropriate gear and drive on smoothly. Encourage them to pick up speed briskly.

If possible, park near a roundabout and observe the traffic as it approaches and negotiates the roundabout. Point out the speed at which vehicles approach, and the size of gap they take. Make sure the learner appreciates the high proportion of drivers who do not signal or position their vehicles correctly – never assume a vehicle is actually doing what its driver is signalling. Ask the learner where they think any particular vehicle is going. Did it signal and position itself correctly? Did it go where they expected?

Start practising on medium size, quiet roundabouts. Some industrial estates or suburban areas may have suitable roundabouts. Concentrate at first on the speed of approach and gear selection. Make sure they are always prepared to stop if necessary, but encourage them to keep moving, no matter how slowly, if possible.

Practise taking the various exits in the following order: first exit (left); last exit (right); and finally straight ahead or any other intermediate exit.

Gaining confidence

Try practising on busier roundabouts and mini-roundabouts. Remember that no left signal is required when leaving a mini-roundabout. Ask the learner to say aloud whether they think there is a suitable gap and either confirm or refute their decision before allowing them to move onto the roundabout.

Ready for the test

Choose a relatively quiet period to practise larger roundabouts. Try to practise roundabouts with lane markings, faster approach roads, traffic lights and any unusual roundabouts in your area. If you have any multiple roundabouts near you, it will be well worth practising these – examiners are likely to include them in test routes if possible.

TROUBLESHOOTING: ROUNDABOUTS

Symptom	Cause	Remedy
ON THE APPROACH		
Too fast	Starting MSM/PSL late	Ensure they start as soon as they can read the map road sign for a roundabout ahead.
	Not braking adequately	Ensure they use progressive braking, prompt with 'Squeeze the brake pedal smoothly.'
	Selecting the wrong gear or changing down too early	Before they start braking, ask what speed and gear they intend to use.
	Coasting (holding the clutch down)	Make sure they brake to the right speed *before* changing down, and only then change gear.
	Starting to brake late	Braking should start as they are level with the map sign.
Too slow	Starting MSM/PSL before they can read the map sign	Ask them what the road number is (e.g. A11). Don't let them slow down before they can answer.
	Over-braking	Make sure they squeeze the brake pedal gently, telling them to 'ease off' the brake if necessary.
Choosing incorrect lane	Uncertain of the rules	Immediately after giving them the directions, ask them which lane they intend to use.
Selecting incorrect gear	Usually rushing or approaching too fast	Ask them what gear they will need as they are slowing down.
Drifting out of position	Not looking forward	Remind them to look where they are going as well as looking for a gap.
	Hands following eyes	Remind them that they will tend to steer where they look, so they must look where they are going.
Stopping unnecessarily	Not looking to the right early enough	Make sure the approach speed is slow enough to complete the whole sequence. Ask, 'Is the roundabout busy?' as they begin braking.
	Looking at vehicles rather than gaps	Ask them if they can see any gaps coming. Prompt them by saying 'There's a big gap after the red car.'
	Not looking for 'blockers'	Remind them to look ahead as well as to the right. Look for vehicles signalling to enter the road you are leaving.
Going when it is not safe	Inadequate observation	Ensure they are slow enough to make effective observations. Make sure they look all the way to the right and ahead. On smaller roundabouts, ask them 'Is that gap big enough?'

TROUBLESHOOTING: ROUNDABOUTS

Symptom	Cause	Remedy
ON THE ROUNDABOUT		
Drifting out of position	Failing to look where they are going	Make sure they look at the lane markings or kerbs in order to maintain position.
	Over- or-under-steering	Make sure their speed is slow enough to steer accurately, and that they use the 'pull push' technique.
Too slow	Insufficient acceleration when joining	Encourage them to '*squeeze* the gas pedal gently', and make sure the clutch comes up smoothly.
Too fast	Approach speed too fast	See above.
	Too much acceleration	'Squeeze the gas pedal gently.'
Signalling poorly timed	Misuse of MSM/PSL routine	Encourage them to say the routine aloud.
	Not counting off the exits as they pass them	Encourage them to count aloud. Check they count only the exits, not the entries.
Changing lanes inappropriately	Uncertain of the rules for lane discipline	Remind them to stay in their lane.
Taking the wrong exit	Not counting off the exits as they pass them	Encourage them to count aloud. Check they count only the exits, not the entries.
	Confusing left and right	Remind them that their left-hand forefinger and thumb make an 'L', or that they write with their right hand (as long as they do).
Exiting into the right-hand lane inappropriately	Forgetting the 'keep left' rule	Remind them of the general rule of the road: 'keep left'.
	Misinterpreting view in left mirror	Make sure they also check their left shoulder to confirm the view in the mirror.

12 Starting on a Hill or at an Angle

What the learner needs to be able to do

They must be able to move away safely and under full control on a level road, on a hill or at an angle from behind a parked vehicle. They must not roll backwards or get too close to any obstructions, and they should keep the car under control without stalling or causing the car to judder or the engine to race. They must make careful observations before moving, taking particular care to check the blind spots.

How to do it

Moving away normally was dealt with in Chapter 2. When moving away on a hill or at an angle the Preparation–Observation–Manoeuvre (POM) routine needs to be modified slightly.

Moving off facing uphill

Before preparing to move off they should use the mirrors to see if there is a suitable gap in sight. Only if there is should they start the preparation phase. If there is no gap in sight, they should delay the preparation and wait in neutral with their feet off the pedals until a suitable gap is visible.

Preparation

They should then prepare the car as for a normal move away, except that they will need to set the gas so that the engine is revving a little more than normal. They will also need to bring the clutch up a little higher than normal when finding biting point. The nose of the car should rise as they find bite – they need to make sure it has risen as far as it will go.

They should avoid holding biting point any longer than is absolutely necessary, as the extra revs and firmer biting point will cause much more wear to the clutch mechanism.

Observation

The observation phase is exactly the same as on the flat, although they need to be aware that on a steep hill they will need a bigger gap, as it will take them slightly longer to get up to speed.

Manoeuvre

When they release the handbrake it will take a little longer for the car to pick up speed, so they will need to hold their feet still for a moment longer. They should feel the engine smooth out before bringing the clutch all the way up and accelerating away.

Moving off facing downhill

Preparation

There is no need to set any gas to move away downhill, so the routine becomes:

- clutch down, select first gear (on a very steep incline they could select second gear);
- apply the footbrake firmly and release the handbrake.

Observation

Exactly as for the flat, finishing off by checking the right blind spot.

Manoeuvre

They should release the footbrake and allow the car to start to roll forward. As soon as they start to move they should move their right foot to the gas and simultaneously bring the clutch up smoothly. The movement of their feet should be smooth and timed as if they were changing gear.

Moving away at an angle

When moving away from behind a parked car, they need to make sure that they give adequate clearance and make frequent observations to their right and ahead, checking for traffic approaching them.

Preparation

Exactly the same as normal:

- clutch down, select first gear, set a little gas and find biting point.

Observation

Their view ahead will be partially obscured by the parked car, so they will need to move in their seat to get a better view. They may also need to indicate, as they may not be able to see clearly enough to be sure that there is no oncoming traffic: the signal will alert such traffic that the learner intends to pull out. They must be particularly careful of pedestrians or other vehicles beyond the obstruction. They must also bear in mind that they will need a bigger gap than normal, as they will be pulling out more slowly than usual.

Manoeuvre

When they are sure it is safe, as far as they can see, they should release the handbrake and keep their feet still. Instead of 'pedalling' normally they will keep the car moving slowly using clutch control. They must immediately steer briskly to the right and check their right blind spot again. As they continue to emerge they must keep looking up and down the road using blind spot checks or mirrors, as the angle dictates. They should still be using clutch control to maintain a slow speed.

When they are sure they are clear of the parked car they should steer briskly to the left to straighten out in the road. They should be prepared to brake in case a pedestrian steps out in front of the parked car.

One final check of the main mirror is necessary to check that it is safe to proceed.

If safe, they should accelerate away smoothly.

Practice plan

First steps

Practise the procedure for a downhill start with the engine off. They should aim to be fluent and smooth. When you are satisfied that they are ready, practise on hills, gradually working from slight inclines to steep slopes where they can start in second gear.

To practise uphill starts, begin by revising the normal move away procedure and gradually introduce steeper inclines. For now, avoid starting in front of other vehicles and be ready to use the handbrake if you start to roll backwards. Make sure that they are looking forwards as they begin the manoeuvre; if they are looking down, they may not notice that they are rolling backwards.

To practise moving away at an angle, start by pulling out from behind a builder's skip or a parked trailer, rather than other cars.

Gaining confidence

Practise hill starts in traffic. Try to find some junctions on hills so that they can practise moving away on a hill and steering at the same time.

Practise moving away at an angle from behind parked cars. Start with a good gap between you – at least one car length – and gradually get closer until you cannot see any tarmac between you.

Ready for the test

Combine the two exercises, so that they practise moving away at an angle on a hill, both up and down the gradient. Try to find some busy junctions or traffic lights on steep hills. They will only build their self-confidence by proving to themselves that they can control the car fully.

TROUBLESHOOTING: STARTING ON A HILL OR AT AN ANGLE		
Symptom	**Cause**	**Remedy**
Rolling backwards	Insufficient gas for the gradient	Only experience will allow them to accurately set the gas, so at first you will need to advise them on the correct amount of gas to use.
	Clutch not high enough	Make sure they make the car's nose rise as far as it will go. Ask 'Have you got a firm enough bite?'
	Not noticing they are on a hill	Ask 'Is the road level or are we on a gradient?'
Jerking forwards	Not keeping the clutch still	Remind them to 'Keep your feet still.'
	Too much gas for the gradient	As for insufficient gas above.
Not moving forwards (uphill)	Clutch not high enough	Ask them to 'Bring the clutch up one millimetre more.'
Not moving forwards (downhill)	Forgetting to release handbrake	As they are making their observations, check to see if the handbrake is off.
Not using footbrake (downhill)	Memory lapse	Remind them to use the footbrake.
Coasting (downhill)	Not bringing the clutch up promptly	Remind them to 'Bring the clutch up smoothly.'
Jerky start (downhill)	Holding the clutch down too long	When the clutch does come back up the car may slow down suddenly. Remind them as above.

13 Other Types of Roads

What the learner needs to be able to do

They need to be able to drive safely on any type of road. So far we have mainly concerned ourselves with ordinary single-carriageway roads. In this chapter we shall look at the how they must modify their driving on dual carriageways, single track roads and one-way roads.

How to do it

Dual carriageways

The learner must be able to recognise the particular features of a dual carriageway and to identify the start and end points in practice. For a road to be classed as a dual carriageway it must consist of two separate roads, usually running parallel, separated by a physical barrier of some sort, such as a metal rail or a grassed area. The number of lanes in each direction is immaterial, but there are usually two or more. Unless otherwise signed, the speed limit on a dual carriageway is 70mph.

Joining

The learner should use the acceleration lane or slip road to build up their speed to match that of the traffic on the dual carriageway. At the end of the barrier, before the end of the slip road, they should start the MSM/PSL routine.

Mirrors – make sure no-one is attempting to overtake them on the slip road.

Signal – they must indicate right to show their intention to join. Many on-slips also double as off-slips, so the signal is essential.

Position – they should stay in their normal road position until it is safe to move closer to the line between the slip road and the main carriageway.

Speed – they must adjust their speed to match that of the traffic already on the dual carriageway – either accelerate or slow down, to avoid travelling abreast of another vehicle.

Look – they should use their right door mirror to look for a safe gap in the traffic, and only when they are fairly certain it is safe they should check over their right shoulder to make sure there is nothing in their blind spot. Only when they are 100% certain it is safe to do so, they should steer very slightly right to drift into the space in the left-hand lane of the dual carriageway. They must not cross the hatched or shaded area, or any solid white lines, but must wait until there is a broken white line.

TIP
Having joined the dual carriageway, they should stay in the left lane long enough to get used to the faster speeds.

On the dual carriageway

Encourage them to look further ahead than usual, normally at least half a mile. At 70mph that is a little over twenty seconds away. They should use scanning techniques to monitor the situation ahead and to the rear; frequent use of the mirrors is essential.

They should:

- be in the left hand lane except when overtaking;
- travel at the speed limit for their vehicle if it is safe to do so, overtaking slower moving traffic as necessary;
- avoid using the brakes unless absolutely necessary – if they look far enough ahead they should be able to adjust their speed sufficiently by use of engine braking alone;
- keep using the Two-second Rule (see page 72) to maintain a safe gap between them and the vehicle ahead (this must be at least doubled in the wet);
- look out for slip roads, pulling out into the next lane or slowing slightly to allow traffic to join from the slip road.

Leaving

They should look out for the signs warning that their exit is near, usually around half a mile away, and on reaching the countdown boards – 300m, 200m and 100m away – they should start the MSM/PSL routine.

Mirrors – check the main and left mirrors.

Signal – indicate left to show that they intend to leave the main carriageway.

Position – at the start of the slip road, they should check their left door mirror again and steer gently into the slip road.

Speed – only when they are in the slip road should they slow down. Keep an eye on the speedometer to make sure they are slowing down enough; it may appear to them that they are going much more slowly than they actually are.

Look – look ahead for the next junction, paying particular attention to vehicles in front that might slow down suddenly.

TIP

After leaving a dual carriageway, they must be very careful with their speed. It will take several minutes for their speed perception to readjust to the slower speeds and they may be going much faster than they think.

Single track roads

These are roads that are not wide enough for two vehicles to pass at once. They are usually found in rural areas where there may also be high hedges and tight bends, so extra care is required.

- The learner must follow the Golden Rule for speed (see page 72) and make sure that they slow down when their view ahead is limited.
- Most single track roads have marked passing places. On seeing another vehicle coming towards them, the learner should continue onwards until there is only one passing place left between the two vehicles. The first vehicle to reach this passing place must stop and pull well in to the left to allow the other vehicle to pass.
- The learner should use the passing places to allow following traffic to overtake them.
- They should be considerate to drivers of large vehicles and traffic coming uphill, letting them through whenever they can.
- They should not try to keep in to the left, but should drive in the middle of the road so that they can see and be seen more easily.
- They must take care when visibility is limited by high hedges or tight bends: they should use the horn to warn other road users of their presence. At night they can use flashed lights to give a similar warning.

One-way roads

- They must travel in the direction shown by the blue-and-white signs.
- They should look out for contra-flow lanes for cyclists or buses. Other than these, they should not have to worry about oncoming traffic.
- They should drive in the most appropriate lane for the direction they intend to take at the end of the one-way system: use the left-hand lane if they intend to go left or straight on, and the right-hand lane if they intend to turn right.
- When turning right off a one-way street, they should position the car well to the right as soon as possible.

- It is permissible to overtake on the left, so they must take care, traffic could be passing on either side.
- They must not reverse in a one-way road except in the course of a normal manoeuvre. It is an offence to reverse any further than necessary, so they may not reverse through a one-way section to effect a short-cut.
- They must look out for signs indicating the end of a one-way system and make sure that they return to the correct side of the road.

Practice plan

First steps

Find a relatively quiet period to practise joining and leaving a dual carriageway for the first time. Practise accelerating to an appropriate speed when joining, and slowing down effectively when leaving the main carriageway. If you intend to follow a section of dual carriageway by leaving and coming straight back on again, take care at the roundabouts or junctions as you leave: the road system designers were not expecting people to do this and it can be difficult to get into the appropriate lane. Doing a complete circuit of the roundabout may make it easier.

Practise using one-way streets. Make sure that they pay particular attention to the signs and markings and that they know what they all mean.

Gaining confidence

Practise joining and leaving dual carriageways, and stay on long enough to practise overtaking. If there is a location where you can join at a T-junction, make sure you practise that.

If you have any single track roads in your area, practise using passing places. Try to practise any sections with tight bends, reminding them to warn others of your presence when thay cannot see very far ahead.

Practise driving in longer one-way systems, such as are often found in town centres. Make sure that they look out for signs and markings indicating the use of lanes.

Ready for the test

They should be confident joining and leaving the dual carriageway by now. Try to find junctions where the slip roads are either unusually short or long. Make sure they practise interchanges between two dual carriageways if possible.

Make sure they are familiar with any one-way systems in your area. Practise driving through gyratory systems (huge roundabouts which are really one-way systems with traffic lights and lanes) if there are any near you.

14 Reversing

What the learner needs to be able to do

They need to be able to reverse in a straight line and around a corner, either to the left or to the right. When reversing, they must keep the rear wheel reasonably close and parallel to the kerb. They must give way to any other road users and make sure that their observations are mainly to the rear of the vehicle, in the direction they are moving.

How to do it

Reversing in a straight line

Find a long straight section of road to practise on. Ask the learner to park on the left, parallel to the kerb but further away than usual, around 20–30cm from the kerb. If necessary, remind them to use the MSM/PSL routine.

Once they are safely parked, ask them to look over their left shoulder at the position of the kerb at the bottom edge of the rear window. There may be a sticker or head-restraint that will act as a reminder. They must remember the exact position of the kerb on the rear window, as this is their reference point to tell them when they are straight.

Remind them that they should adjust their sitting position to enable them to see clearly through the rear window, and that they are allowed to remove their seat belt when reversing.

Preparation

They should prepare the car as normal, this time using reverse gear and using only a little gas.

Observation

They must look all the way around the car, finishing by checking the right blind spot before looking through the rear window in the direction they intend to go.

Manoeuvre

When they are sure it is safe to proceed, they should release the handbrake and keep the car moving very slowly in a straight line, parallel to the kerb. To do this they should keep the kerb on the reference point they established when they first stopped, steering gently in the same direction if the kerb moves off that point.

They must maintain all-round observations while moving and must come to a stop if anything approaches closer than about 20m. If they do have to stop, they should keep their right foot on the footbrake so that the brake lights are illuminated.

When they have reversed as far as you intended, ask them to brake to a stop, apply the handbrake and select neutral. Only then should they turn their body to face forwards again.

Reversing into a side road on the left

This manoeuvre begins and ends with a straight reverse – the new skill here is to steer accurately around the corner.

Approach

Ask them to pull over and park on the left before the side road they will be reversing into. Make sure that the side road is clearly visible, but they should not be so close as to obstruct the junction in any way. Tell them that you want them to reverse into the next side road on the left.

- They should pull away properly and drive slowly past the junction. As they pass it they should look into the side road to check for obstructions and also to assess the sharpness of the corner.
- If it is necessary for them to signal to show their intention to pull over and stop, make sure their signal is properly timed and does not mislead others into thinking that they intend to turn into the side road.
- They should stop about 1.5 car lengths past the turning point, and a little further from the kerb than normal (20–30cm). If the corner is very sharp they may need to stop further from the kerb (up to 50cm).

Preparation

They must apply the handbrake and select reverse before cancelling the indicator, if they used it. They will need to swivel in their seat in order to see clearly through the rear window. If they have not turned their body, prompt them by asking if they can see clearly through the rear window.

Observation

They should make all-round obser-vations and check it is safe to proceed.

Manoeuvre

When it is safe, they should reverse straight back slowly, using clutch control, checking the right blind spot before they reach the turning point.

- If the corner is sweeping they should steer towards the kerb using half a turn of the steering wheel.
- If the corner is sharp they should use one complete turn of the wheel.

This initial turn will cause the nose to swing out into the road. You must be prepared to stop them if they have not made adequate observations.

- As they follow the corner they must be looking mainly through the rear window, in the direction they are moving.

- They must also check all around the car at regular intervals, as well as checking their position relative to the kerb in the left door mirror.
- They must not stare in the left door mirror.

Each time they glance in the mirror they should be assessing their position relative to the kerb and adjusting their steering. Track the car's position yourself and check that they steer the correct way without over-steering.

TIP

You may need to stop them and prompt them by asking 'How far across the mirror is the kerb?' If they answer 'Halfway', then they should have the steering wheel about half a turn towards the kerb. If they answer 'Three-quarters', the steering wheel should be three-quarters of a turn towards the kerb, and so on. (Full details of how to use the door mirror as a steering meter can be found in the AA *Driving Skills Manual*).

As they proceed, make sure that their observations continue to follow the routine. You must also make full observations, and remember that they may miss seeing an approaching pedestrian or vehicle.

TIP

During the manoeuvre it is acceptable for their hands to cross on the steering wheel, or for them to use only one hand if necessary. Make sure, however, that they are always in control; they must always have at least one hand in contact with the wheel.
The preferred grip is to have the right hand at the top of the wheel and the left hand low down.

They should be reversing as slowly as possible. Do not attempt to get them to move faster. Examiners will expect learners to maintain a slow but steady speed, avoiding stopping unnecessarily. The most important consideration is that the manoeuvre is completely safe and controlled; this can only be done at a slow speed.

As they near the end of the corner, they should spot the kerb in the rear window and wait for it to reach the reference point that they established earlier. When the car is straight and parallel to the kerb, they should straighten the wheels and reverse back from the junction to a distance of about three car lengths. Once stopped, they should apply the handbrake and select neutral before facing forwards again.

Before they drive off again, you will need to tell them which way to turn at the junction. Make sure that they make proper observations, including the blind-spot check, and signal only after they have started to move.

TIP

If a vehicle approaches from behind and makes no attempt to pass, you may need to take the initiative and tell the learner what to do. If there is enough room to continue and the other vehicle is obviously waiting, then tell the learner to carry on. Some drivers, however, may pull up right behind you. In this situation, you have no choice other than to abandon the reverse. Ask the learner to pull forwards around the corner and start again when the other vehicle has moved on.

Reversing into a side road on the right

It is exceptionally rare for this manoeuvre to be requested in a driving test, but if you are driving a van where vision through the rear is obscured, this is the preferred option.

Approach

As for the left reverse, you should ask the learner to pull over and park on the left before the road to the right you intend to use. Tell them that you want them to reverse into the side road on the right.

- They should then move off and approach the junction, using the MSM/PSL routine as if they were going to turn right.
- When level with the side road, they should check for obstructions, assess the corner and indicate right.
- They should steer over to the right-hand side of the road, about 20–30cm from the kerb, and drive slowly forwards until they are about three car lengths past the junction.

If anything approaches as they do this, they must stop and let them pass before continuing.

Preparation

Select reverse and find biting point.

Observation

They should make careful all-round observations, especially of the left blind spot. They must position themselves in their seat so that they can see clearly behind them.

Manoeuvre

When safe, they should reverse straight back, looking through the rear window. When they are unable to see the kerb in the rear window, they should stop and reposition themselves so that they get a clear view of the kerb over their right shoulder. They can wind down their window and look out if they wish. At the turning point, they should again come to a stop, look all around the car and make sure it is safe.

Looking over their right shoulder, they should steer around the corner using the same technique as for the left reverse. They may look out of their window as they reverse.

When straight in the new road, they should again come to a stop, reposition themselves to look over their left shoulder, through the rear window, and continue to reverse slowly until they are about six car lengths back from the junction. They should then come to a stop and secure the vehicle.

They should wait for your instructions, then select first gear and make full all-round observations, finishing by checking the left blind spot. When it is safe, they should move off and steer briskly back to the normal side of the road and immediately start the MSM/PSL routine for the junction.

Practice plan

First steps

Find a long, straight section of quiet road where you can practise the straight reverse. Shifting in their seat may cause the learner's clutch control to suffer, so concentrate at first on maintaining a very slow speed.

Practise the left reverse on a quiet road where you are unlikely to be interrupted by other vehicles. Start with sweeping corners and make sure the learner is making effective observations. Encourage them to get into a rhythm and act appropriately on any hazards they see.

Gaining confidence

When practising the straight reverse, get them to deliberately start from an awkward position and practise getting back to a good position as quickly as they can. Ask them to start a long way from the kerb or at quite a sharp angle. Practise reversing on a mixture of sweeping and sharp corners to the left.

Make sure you find a very quiet area to practise the right reverse. Don't dwell too much on this, as it is very unlikely they will need to use it either during the test or in 'real life'.

Ready for the test

Concentrate on practising the left reverse. As well as practising a mixture of sharp and sweeping corners, practise reversing into side roads on hills, into side roads of various widths and those in busier areas. Where possible, practise reversing further than normal into the side road, so you are adding an extra straight reverse to the end of the left reverse. They may need to do this if there is a car parked in the side road, in order to make room for other vehicles to pass easily.

Avoid very busy areas; rule 176 of *The Highway Code* specifically advises you to avoid such areas.

TROUBLESHOOTING: REVERSING		
Symptom	**Cause**	**Remedy**
Too fast	Poor clutch control	Practise clutch control exercises (see Chapter 3) before practising straight reverse again.
Stopping unnecessarily	Poor clutch control	See above.
Hitting or too close to the kerb	Over-steering	Make sure the learner only adjusts the steering by a quarter turn at a time.
	Left mirror set incorrectly (angled in too much)	Readjust mirror so that the learner can see the top of the rear wheel arch and just a bit of the side of the car.
	Not spotting reference point on rear window	Before reversing, remind the learner to check the reference point. If there are consistent problems, use a letter on the dealer's sticker or apply a sticky dot in the correct position to act as a reminder.
Too far from the kerb	Under-steering	Check that the learner makes positive adjustments to the steering when necessary; each adjustment should be about a quarter turn of the wheel.
	Mirror set incorrectly (angled out too much)	See above.
Steering the wrong way	Poor spatial ability	This is a very common problem, so be patient. Try using 'towards the kerb' or 'away from the kerb' instead of left and right. Talk them through using the format: 'Where does the kerb touch the bottom of the mirror?', 'You need to turn towards/away from the kerb.'
Vehicles or pedestrians approaching unseen	Inadequate observations	Make sure that the learner uses a routine for their observations. They must look mainly backwards, but must also make frequent glances in every other direction as well.
Revving engine	Too much gas set or lack of control	They should only need enough gas set to ensure that the engine runs smoothly – no more than they would use when moving away normally on the same road.

15 Parking

What the learner needs to be able to do

The learner will need to be able to carry out two parking exercises: parallel parking (parking parallel to the kerb between two parked cars) and bay parking (reversing into a marked bay). Only one of these exercises may be requested during the Driving Test.

How to do it

Parallel parking

The learner should use the POM routine (as for moving away) to guide them through the manoeuvre.

They should approach the parked vehicle in front of the space slowly and stop alongside it, about 1m away and slightly forward.

Preparation – they should select reverse and find biting point, using very little gas.

Observation – they must make all-round observations, waiting if necessary for other vehicles to pass or come to a complete stop.

Manoeuvre – they must be looking through the rear window as they start to reverse slowly. As soon as they are moving they should check their right blind spot. When their rear seat is level with the other car's bumper, they should turn in to the space by making one complete turn of the steering wheel towards the kerb.

They must again glance all around the car, making sure it is safe. As they turn in to the space, they should alternate their observations between the rear window and the left door mirror. At the instant the kerbstones disappear from the left mirror, they should make two turns away from the kerb.

As the nose of the car swings in towards the kerb, they must take care not to let the car speed up as the wheels run down the camber of the road. As they look through the rear window they will see the kerb moving across towards their reference point. The instant that they are straight they must straighten the wheels briskly and come to a stop, apply the handbrake and select neutral. If there is a car behind them, they may not be able to see the kerb in the rear window. In such a case, they may use the door mirror to see when they are straight, but must remember to look through the rear window as much as possible.

Making corrections

If they consistently finish too far from the kerb (that is, more than 20cm) or keep running onto the kerb, there are a number of possible reasons.

Too far away:

- steering away from the kerb too soon, not waiting until the kerb disappears from the mirror;
- steering away from the kerb too quickly – the steering wheel should go around at the same speed as the road wheels;
- moving too slowly – the car should move at a slow but steady speed;
- left door mirror may be incorrectly positioned.

Too close:

- steering away from the kerb too late, missing the point at which the kerb disappears;
- steering away from the kerb too slowly; the speed of the steering and road wheels should match;
- moving too fast, failing to keep the car moving slowly, maybe running down the camber of the road;
- left door mirror may be incorrectly positioned.

Bay parking on the right

They should approach the bay slowly and maintain their normal road position, 1m from the left-hand edge of the road. If there are parked cars on their left, they must leave enough room for the nose to swing out as they turn into the bay. The chosen bay is 'bay one'. They should drive slowly forward past bays one, two and three, until the line separating bays three and four is level with their shoulder. At this point, stop and begin the POM routine:

Preparation – select reverse and find biting point.

Observation – make all-round observations to ensure it is safe.

Manoeuvre – looking through the rear window they should start to reverse slowly, and immediately steer towards the chosen bay until they reach full lock. Make sure they turn the steering wheel at the same speed as the road wheels are turning.

They should check the front left corner, making sure they do not get too close to any cars parked on the left, and then look over their right shoulder to check that they are steering around the white line to the right of bay one. As they reverse they should keep looking around every few seconds, stopping if necessary for approaching vehicles.

When they are nearly in the bay, the white line on their right will disappear from view, below the window sill. At this point they need to use the left door mirror to look for the line on their left. As soon as they see this line they should straighten the wheels. If the car is not straight in the bay, they will need to steer about half a turn in the same direction as they are pointing, until they are straight again. They must then look over their left shoulder to see how far back they can go, and complete the reverse.

Bay parking on the left

As before they should approach the bay slowly, stopping when the far line of the chosen bay is level with their shoulder. They must check all around to see that it is safe and then move slowly forwards, steering briskly to full-right lock. At an angle of about 45°, they should stop, apply the handbrake and select reverse.

They should again make all-round observations before reversing and simultaneously steering to full-left lock. They should keep checking both sides of the car as they reverse slowly into the bay. When they are straight they should straighten the wheels and reverse fully into the bay, then stop and secure the car.

Entering a bay forwards

This is actually harder than reversing in, as the car is more manoeuvrable in reverse. They need to approach on the opposite side of the road to their chosen bay, so it makes sense to choose one on the right if possible. As they near the bay, they should make all-round observation. If turning into a bay on the left they should steer to the right-hand side of the road and get the car straight. If entering a bay on their right they should continue in their normal position.

When the nose of the car is level with the nearest white line of the chosen bay, they should steer briskly into the bay. They should keep checking their position relative to other vehicles and keep the car moving slowly. When they are fully inside the space they should stop, apply the handbrake and select neutral.

Practice plan

First steps

Practise the parallel park on a wide road, so that you won't have to worry about blocking the road, and behind just one car. Practising the bay park is more difficult, as many supermarkets ban learner drivers from their land. Try to find a big car park with plenty of empty areas where you won't upset anyone.

Gaining confidence

Practise the parallel park on normal roads. Practise bay parking, both right and left, in spaces surrounded by other vehicles. Make sure they also practise entering the bay nose first.

Ready for the test

Make sure that they practise parallel parking behind vehicles of various sizes, and practise parking into smaller gaps. As long as the gap is at least 1.5 times the length of your car you should be able to get in.

16 Turning in the Road

What the learner needs to be able to do

The learner needs to be able to turn the car around in the road, using forward and reverse gears. They must make effective all-round observations and keep full control of the car's speed and steering.

How to do it

The 'turn in the road' is often misleadingly referred to as the 'three-point turn'. On a narrower road they may need to take five turns, depending on the car's turning circle and length. The turn consists of three (or five) 'move away' and 'stop' movements, and the POM (Preparation–Observation–Manoeuvre) routine used when moving away.

First Turn

Preparation – they should prepare the car as normal, but use a small amount of gas, as they will be using clutch control to keep the car moving as slowly as possible.

Observation – they must make all-round observations, giving way to any approaching vehicle.

Manoeuvre – when it is safe to do so, they should release the handbrake and move slowly forward, steering right to full lock as briskly as they can. They must make good use of clutch and brake control to keep the car moving slowly, taking into account the camber of the road. Make sure they don't 'dry steer' – that is, turn the steering wheel when the car is stationary.

When they can see the kerb appear underneath their door mirror they should steer briskly to the left and, at the same time, gently brake to a stop. They must apply the handbrake and select neutral.

Second Turn

Preparation – they should then depress the clutch and select reverse. Set a little gas and find biting point.

Observation – make sure that they make full observations and look through the rear window before and as they start to move.

Manoeuvre – when it is safe, they should release the handbrake and move slowly backwards, steering briskly to full-left lock. As soon as the car is straight across the road, at right angles to the kerb, they should look over their right shoulder, watching for the point at which the kerb moves into the nearest corner of the rear passenger's window, by the door pillar.

TIP

The exact position of this point, and the exact position where the kerb appears under the door mirror on the previous turn, will vary from car to car.

At this point they should turn briskly to the right and gently brake to a stop, apply the handbrake and select neutral.

Third Turn

Preparation – they should prepare the car as before.

Observation – they must make all round observations.

Manoeuvre – when it is safe, they should release the handbrake and steer right to return to the normal side of the road. On the Driving Test the examiner will probably ask them to drive on as they reach the other side, but when practising you should ask them to pull over and park on the left – you may want to debrief them or have another go.

Five turns

If the road is too narrow to complete the manoeuvre in three moves, they should repeat the second and third turns.

Giving way

When carrying out the 'turn in the road' manoeuvre, they must give way to any other traffic. If any vehicle approaches they should finish the turn they are making and stop as normal. They should prepare the car in the usual way and then look to see if the other vehicle is going to wait. If they choose to wait, the learner should continue the manoeuvre. If the other vehicle chooses to pass, the learner must give way.

TIP

The key to carrying out this manoeuvre successfully is to make sure that they move very slowly but steer briskly. Good clutch control is essential, as is good observation – they must always look in the direction they are moving.

Practice plan

First steps

Practise on a fairly wide but quiet road, where they will certainly be able to manage the manoeuvre in three moves.

Gaining confidence

Practise on narrower roads where they will have to make five turns.

Ready for the test

Practise on a mixture of wide and narrow roads, including some with very steep cambers, on hills and on poorly surfaced roads.

17 Keeping Space

What the learner needs to be able to do

They must always make sure that they have sufficient space around the vehicle. That means they must maintain a safe gap between themselves and the vehicle in front, space to the sides of the vehicle so that they do not get too close to other road users, and they should try to ensure an adequate distance behind them.

How to do it

When moving

Ahead

The first rule concerns the space in front of the car. The **Two-second Rule** tells the learner that they should maintain a gap of at least two seconds between them and the vehicle in front. Check this by noting a fixed point ahead, such as an arrow on the road, a road sign or a streetlamp, and start saying *'Only a fool breaks the Two-second Rule'* as the vehicle in front passes that point. It takes about two seconds to say the phrase, and you should be able to complete it before your vehicle reaches the same point. If the learner can't complete the phrase, they need to slow down slightly and let the gap ahead increase.

TIP

If you are good at judging distances, this works out at around 1m for every 1mph of speed.

On wet roads, they must at least double this gap, as it would take longer to stop in an emergency. In icy conditions they should increase this gap further to at least 10 times the amount of space.

The learner should use the **Golden Rule for speed**: *always drive at such as speed that you can comfortably stop in the distance ahead you can see to be safe.* They should never get closer than the overall stopping distance for the speed they are going.

TIP

Remember, at night they will need to drive more slowly, as the distance ahead they can see to be safe is limited to the range of the headlights.

Behind

If a vehicle is driving too closely behind, the learner must increase the gap in front. This is to allow time to give more warning if they are going to slow down. By increasing the gap in front to include the gap for the following vehicle as well, they create

time to just show their brake lights before they start to brake more firmly. This should give the other driver time to slow down before the learner does.

Persistent tailgaters cause extreme danger to others. The learner should indicate left, slow down and let them pass; they are much safer with the tailgater in front where they can be seen more easily.

Sides

The general rule for positioning the car is that you should always be 1m from the side of the road or any obstruction you need to pass. This 1m gap is a safety margin in case a pedestrian steps off the pavement or a car noses out over the Give Way line at a junction. If the learner is forced to get closer than 1m from the kerb, then they must slow down.

They should:

- maintain this 1m gap when passing parked cars or other obstructions;
- allow at least a 1m gap on the right-hand side of the car, never getting closer to oncoming traffic than is absolutely necessary;
- never drive in another driver's blind spot. This is particularly important on dual carriageways. They should drop back so that they can see the other drivers' eyes in his or her door mirror; that way they know the other driver can see them. A similar rule applies when following large vehicles, such as lorries or coaches – if you can't see their mirrors, they can't see you;
- avoid driving alongside, or abreast of, another vehicle;
- leave space to improve their view and allow room for manoeuvre.

They should drive with an imaginary bubble around the vehicle. If they have space all around, they have more options should they ever need to take emergency action, and more time to avoid ever having to take such action.

When stationary

- They should use the **Tyres and Tarmac rule**: *always stop far enough behind the vehicle in front so that you can see their tyres touching the road and 1m of tarmac*. This space leaves room to comfortably pull out and pass should the vehicle ahead break down. It also leaves room to manoeuvre out of the way if an emergency vehicle needs to pass. It will also leave room to react if the vehicle in front rolls back at a junction.
- They should never stop so that they block access to a side road or business entrance.

- If they have to stop alongside a parked car, they should allow room for the other driver to open their door.
- When in queuing traffic, they must never stop on a pedestrian crossing. This is doubly important for level crossings or marked tramways – the train or tram won't be able to stop.
- When parking, they should make sure they do not block access to driveways or side roads.
- They should not park opposite bus stops unless there is plenty of room for vehicles to pass between them and a bus waiting at the stop.
- They should never park too close to a vehicle showing a disabled badge; the occupants may need room to put a wheelchair in the boot.

Practice plan

First steps

Practise using the Two-second Rule. Using it consistently will give them much more time to assess situations and avoid hurried reactions, resulting in smoother and more comfortable driving. They must remember to multiply the time by two or ten in wet or icy weather.

Gaining confidence

In queuing traffic, practise the Tyres and Tarmac rule. Make sure they use this as a guide whenever they pull up behind another vehicle.

Ready for the test

On dual carriageways or other multi-lane roads, practise avoiding driving in the blind spots or abreast of other vehicles. Make sure they are conscious of their position relative to other vehicles, and remind them to make sure that other drivers can see them.

Practise the Two-second Rule on faster roads to see how much bigger the gap needs to be.

Regularly ask the learner to 'Pull over and park on the left', especially in busier areas. This will give them practice in finding suitable parking places.

18 Use of Speed

What the learner needs to be able to do

The learner must always make sure that they are driving at an appropriate speed for the road and traffic conditions. When it is safe to do so, they should travel at the speed limit, making progress and not holding up other road users. They must be able to recognise situations where it would not be safe to travel at the speed limit and adjust their speed accordingly.

Dangers of speed: what they need to know

The learner must appreciate the dangers of travelling too fast and recognise that speed limits are just that – limits not targets. They should be aware of the legal penalties for speeding, but much more importantly they must be aware of the danger to themselves and others. In the AA *Driving Skills Manual* the learner will find some shocking statistics relating to the use of speed. It is vital that they appreciate the danger of speeding, and learn to use speed sensibly and with consideration for others.

How to do it

Hazard awareness

As part of their Theory Test, learners will have to take a test of hazard perception. This is an important skill which must be developed at every opportunity. It is also the basis for the two methods of ensuring that they drive at a speed appropriate to the road and traffic conditions.

Method for driving in built-up areas

On 30mph roads they must slow down for any hazard they see. They should take 5mph off the speed limit for each and every hazard.

The table on the next page gives examples of the sorts of hazards they might come across. According to this, if they were driving on a dark, rainy afternoon, weaving their way through the parked cars outside the local school as the children are coming out, then they should be reversing away from the area at 5mph. It is obviously silly to take the system to that extreme, but this is a scenario many drivers face on a daily basis in the winter. Realistically, they should slow down to around no more than 15mph or even 10mph if they need to negotiate tight spaces between parked cars. At 15mph an alert driver would be able to stop in less than one car length.

DRIVING IN RESIDENTIAL OR BUILT-UP AREAS	
HAZARD	**SUBTRACT**
Residential or urban area	**5mph**
Pedestrians around	**5mph**
Children around	**5mph**
Parked cars on your side of the road	**5mph**
Parked cars on other side of the road	**5mph**
In the dark	**5mph**
Adverse weather conditions	**5mph**

By reducing their speed by 5mph for every additional hazard, they are creating time and space to deal with the various possible dangers.

- In a busy town centre pedestrians could step off the kerb to avoid obstructions, or cross the road unexpectedly.
- Schoolchildren are unpredictable and can move very fast. They may playfully push their friends into the road and catch them at the last moment ('Tell your mum I saved you!'). What if they miss the catch?
- The door of a parked car could swing open as they pass, or the driver might pull away without checking their blind spot. The car could also hide a child stepping out behind it.
- At night it is much more difficult to see pedestrians or cyclists – even those who wear brightly coloured reflective or fluorescent clothing.
- Bad weather can make it much harder to see: driving rain may not be adequately cleared by the windscreen wipers; mist and fog limit the distance drivers can see ahead; snow can be very disorientating; strong wind can affect the steering, and even bright sunshine can temporarily blind a driver and make it impossible to see into the shadows. Consider also that pedestrians are more likely to run with their heads down, or have their visibility reduced by hoods, hats, umbrellas, wet spectacles or eyes screwed up against the light.

You will be able to add to this list with many more from your own experience. Make a point of highlighting any such hazards you see as you are practising; the more the learner experiences, the more carefully they will drive. Every hazard is a potential accident – only by slowing down in case it develops can they be sure they are driving safely. Keep asking them 'What if…?' That way they will be prepared for anything that does happen.

Adapting this for faster roads

On roads with a speed limit higher than 30mph we can modify the above system slightly. As a general rule (though this cannot always be assumed), on main roads it would be safe to drive at the speed limit unless road signs or markings instruct otherwise. To assess the appropriate speed for a major road, take 10mph off the speed limit for every different type of sign you see and for any additional hazards you can see.

Remember, any triangular sign gives a warning of a hazard, and marks a place where they may have to slow down or steer. By slowing down when they first see the warning triangle they are already prepared for the hazard, should it materialise. Watch the learner's eyes whenever you see a warning sign – check that they look at it and take appropriate action.

The positioning of signs is often well planned, so that if they come off the gas a soon as they see the first sign (having checked the mirrors first, of course), then they will only need to brake very gently in order to slow to the appropriate speed. Remember the Golden Rule: *you should always be driving at such a speed that you can stop comfortably in the distance you can see ahead to be safe.*

Method for cornering

The second method is about cornering at the correct speed and has two parts: balancing the weight of the car, and reading the road.

Gripping the road

To keep the weight of the car evenly distributed over all four tyres, the driver must try to keep the centre of gravity as close to the centre of the car as possible. If they slow down to a safe speed and start to accelerate very gently before they start to turn, the weight of the car will be pulled back towards the centre, putting less demand on the front tyres. This not only gives a much more comfortable ride, but is also safer, as the weight of the car is more evenly distributed over the four tyres.

Judging the bend

The second element is to make sure they read the road accurately. It can be very difficult to judge how tight a corner or bend is, so they need to learn to assess the severity of the bend and the correct speed to use.

As they approach the bend they will not be able to see as far ahead and must therefore slow down. They should always look to see how far ahead the vanishing point is – that is, the point at which the two sides of the road appear to meet. For example, when the vanishing point is 50m ahead, they should be travelling no faster than 50mph because the overall stopping distance at 50mph is 53m. If they use this system they can be sure that they are never going too fast for the bend.

When they are at the correct speed for that particular corner, the vanishing point will appear to stay the same distance away. As they steer around the bend the vanishing point will start to get further away as the road straightens out. At this point they can start to accelerate gently out of the bend.

TIP

To practise this, it would help if you drive along a twisty road while the learner watches the vanishing point from the passenger seat.

Practice plan

First steps

Practise spotting hazards as you drive. At first ask them to just say 'hazard!' out loud, then gradually become more specific, saying 'parked car' or 'child on bike'. They should include every road sign they see. If you have seen a sign or hazard which they have not yet mentioned, you must point it out.

Ask them to practise judging distances in metres. They could try estimating the distance from your parked car to a junction, a lamppost or another parked car. Get them to pace it out and see how accurate they are.

They must learn the overall stopping distances from *The Highway Code*, and make sure they know what the speed limits are on various types of roads.

Gaining confidence

Practise spotting hazards as you drive around built-up areas and, for each one, make sure that they check their mirrors and slow down by 5mph to a minimum of around 15mph.

On faster roads, make sure they spot the road signs as soon as you do and that they reduce the maximum speed limit by 10mph for each different sign.

Find a national speed limit road that has a few good bends. Ask them to practise watching the vanishing point and adjust their speed accordingly. It may help them if you drive until they get the hang of this. If necessary, you could describe what the vanishing point is doing as they drive.

Ready for the test

Periodically check that they know what the speed limit is. They should always be right. They should always be driving within the maximum speed limit, making progress when it is safe and reducing their speed when it is not. Make sure that they use the MSM/PSL routine for every hazard they see.

Ask them if they could do a commentary drive – that is, saying out loud everything that they see and what they are doing. They should identify the hazard, say what could happen and explain the actions they are taking in response to that hazard.

Commentary driving has such a dramatic effect on developing driver awareness and planning, it is worth devoting an hour or so to it as they get closer to taking their practical test.

19 Adverse Conditions

What the learner needs to be able to do

They must be able to drive safely in adverse conditions. They should know how to modify their driving to maximise safety and how to operate any controls required to improve visibility. Many of the rules for driving in adverse weather also apply to driving at night.

How to do it

While it is unlikely that you will be able to plan practise sessions in adverse conditions, you should take any opportunity that presents itself. Many learners choose to learn during the late spring or summer and may never take a lesson with their instructor in bad weather or in darkness.

There are two main considerations for the learner in adverse conditions: visibility and control.

Visibility

Whenever visibility is reduced the learner must consider how easily they may be seen and how much they can see. When visibility is less than 100m they must use dipped headlights, and should turn on fog lights too, if they are fitted. When visibility improves beyond 100m they must remember to turn off the fog lights, but may still keep the headlights on. They should always use headlights if any lights are required – sidelights are insufficient for a moving vehicle.

They must use the windscreen wipers when necessary and will need to know how to operate them properly, including the rear wipers and washer controls. Fog and mist will also cause the windscreen to become obscured, but it may be less obvious, especially in daylight.

They must also know how to operate the heating controls in order to clear misted up windows. Make sure they know the particular settings for your car – they may be completely different from their instructor's car.

If the opportunity arises, get them to clear the windscreen and windows of ice on a cold morning. De-icer and a scraper are usually the best way.

They must also make sure that the windscreen washer bottle is topped up and has some sort of anti-freezing agent. When the roads have been gritted they will need to wash the windscreen much more frequently.

Control

They must be aware of how the weather can affect their control of the car. In wet or icy weather they must increase their separation distance – to double or ten times the Two-second Rule (see Chapter 18) respectively.

Ice or snow

- They must reduce their speed and increase the separation distance. Reduced tyre noise may indicate that they are on ice.
- They must drive as smoothly as possible, making no sudden changes of speed or steering.
- They should only brake in a straight line, and should use the highest gear possible for the speed they are doing (20mph in fourth would be reasonable in these conditions).
- They should avoid driving in ruts and must watch out for road maintenance vehicles such as gritting lorries and snowploughs.
- They should tune the radio to a local station for weather information or police advice on driving conditions.

Rain

- They should avoid driving through puddles if possible. Their steering may be pulled towards the kerb, and the puddle may be deeper than they think.
- They must never drive through standing water so fast as to splash pedestrians.
- On faster roads, standing water can cause the car to aquaplane. If they spot the water before they reach it they should slow down. If they do start to aquaplane they should ease off the gas and hold the steering straight without braking. The tyre noise will disappear – but you may not notice this for the noise of the water hitting the bodywork.
- If they must drive through deeper water such as a flood or a ford, they should drive slowly in first gear but with plenty of revs and slipping the clutch to prevent water entering the engine or the exhaust. After passing through the water they should test the brakes by driving slowly and braking gently. If the brakes are affected they can dry them by driving slowly with a little gas and simultaneously applying the brakes very gently with their left foot. (This is the only time that they may ever brake with their left foot.)

Wind

- Strong gusts may blow a car off course and the learner must be especially careful when driving between open and sheltered areas, including passing lorries or bridges.

- They must look out particularly for more vulnerable road users who may be blown around, such as cyclists or motorcyclists, drivers towing trailers or caravans and drivers of high sided vehicles.

- They must also watch out for debris blown by the wind such as fallen branches, roof tiles or even plastic bags (these can get stuck on the windscreen).

Sun

Bright sunshine brings its own inherent problems.

- Heat may cause tarmac to soften, affecting the grip of the tyres.

- Low sun can cause visibility problems and make it difficult to see properly, especially into shaded areas. The learner must slow down and use the sun visor. Wearing sun glasses when the sun is low can cause more problems than it cures, as shadows appear darker, hiding anything that may be in them.

- The effects of low sun will be much worse if the windscreen is dirty. They should use the windscreen washers to clean the outside and if necessary, stop to clean the inside. If they wear spectacles, those must be clean too.

Night driving

- At night the learner must use headlights. They must only use main beam when the road ahead is completely clear, and should be ready to dip the lights whenever they approach a corner.

- The official 'lighting up time' is published in daily papers next to the weather forecast, but the general rule is to turn lights on when the first streetlamps come on, or when they see other vehicles with their lights on.

- On unlit roads their range of vision is limited by the extent of their lights, so they will need to slow down to comply with the Golden Rule for speed.

- It is much harder to see pedestrians, cyclists and animals, so drivers must be much more vigilant. Even in areas with street lighting you may be able to show them how invisible pedestrians become unless they are directly lit by headlights.

- Judging speed and distance at night is much more difficult, so they must take great care at junctions and in meeting situations.

Dazzling

- They should allow a minute or so for their eyes to adjust to the dark before starting to drive. Use this time for a thorough cockpit drill or cleaning the windscreen – clean glass cuts down the dazzle of oncoming lights.
- They should avoid looking directly at oncoming traffic, but focus on the left-hand kerb at the limit of the range of their own lights.
- Make sure they know how and when to operate the anti-dazzle switch on the main mirror, if fitted.
- They should avoid dazzling others, using dipped lights when necessary, and keeping back so that their light beam does not touch the car in front.
- If the headlights on your car are adjustable, make sure the adjuster is set to the appropriate setting, especially if you have rear seat passengers or a heavy load in the boot.
- If they are dazzled, the learner should slow down and stop if necessary. They must not retaliate by using their own main beam.
- When stopped, they should not keep their foot on the footbrake, as the brake lights could dazzle the driver travelling behind.

Parking

- On a 30mph (or less) road, they may park without lights, but must face the same way as the flow of traffic.
- On faster roads they must use sidelights or parking lights.
- Whenever they are parked they must turn off their headlights and use sidelights instead.

Noise

- They must not sound their horn between 11.30pm and 7am except to avoid danger from a moving vehicle.
- They should keep all noise to a minimum at night, avoiding slamming doors or revving the engine.
- If your car is fitted with an alarm make sure they know how to arm and disarm it properly.

Practice plan

As you have no control over the weather you simply must take the opportunity to practise as it arises. Avoid really bad conditions until you are happy with every other aspect of their driving.

20 Vulnerable Road Users

What the learner needs to be able to do

The learner must be able to demonstrate that they are aware of the needs of more vulnerable road users, and that they show them due consideration and drive with their safety in mind at all times. They must be especially careful around cyclists, pedestrians, motorcyclists and horse riders. They should be especially considerate towards learner drivers, emergency vehicles, public transport vehicles and lorries.

How to do it

As an experienced driver, you will be well aware of the many and varied dangers you are likely to meet. Remember that the learner may never have witnessed a child running out in front of them without warning, and, although they are prepared in theory to deal with such situations, they may be caught unawares. As you supervise their practice, it is crucial that you are even more vigilant then normal so that you can instruct the learner to take action if required.

A fuller consideration of dealing with vulnerable road users is given in the AA *Driving Skills Manual*. Here we shall only outline the types of hazards or problems, leaving the details to your own personal experience.

Built-up areas

Pedestrians are most likely to be found in shopping or residential areas. Care must be taken when passing parked vehicles or skips and when near bus stops or railway stations, ice cream or snack vans, schools or playgrounds and when near roundabouts or large junctions.

The learner should be particularly careful when around children, the elderly and people with disabilities.

They must take care around cyclists who may swerve out to avoid a drain cover, or younger cyclists who may not be in full control of their bike. At night they should be particularly vigilant for cyclists without lights or reflective clothing.

Animals

Animals have no road sense and the learner must take care. Horses may be spooked by the sudden noise of an engine, so the learner must slow down and pass as quietly as possible. They should be wary of pets in residential areas and farm animals on country roads. Some areas have their own local specialities, such as deer in woodland areas, or ducks and geese near the village pond. They should be alert for signs such as droppings or manure, riding school signs, or eyes reflecting at night.

The learner should always slow down whenever they suspect there may be animals around. They must not make an emergency stop for small animals, so if they wish to avoid killing something they must drive at such a speed that they could stop if necessary.

Other drivers

As a learner, they should understand the problems other learner drivers can have and they must be patient and considerate. It is well worth reminding them of this even some months after they have passed their test.

Equal consideration must be given to the elderly who may drive more slowly or erratically.

Emergency vehicles must always be given priority. If a siren approaches, the learner should look for the warning lights. If necessary they should pull over and allow the vehicle to pass.

Buses and trams should be given preferential treatment: the learner should allow them to pull out from stops, and should take care when passing them at stops.

Flashing amber lights signify slow-moving, broken down or particularly large vehicles: give them plenty of room to manoeuvre.

Ordinary lorries may also require considerably more room, especially when turning or manoeuvring. The learner should keep well back and give the lorry space to complete their manoeuvre safely.

Practice plan

It is unlikely that you can plan practice sessions dealing with all vulnerable road users, but school opening or closing times may provide the opportunity to practise dealing with children, and a Saturday afternoon session in the town centre will give plenty of practice with pedestrians in general. Animals are less predictable, but make sure you take the learner to any locations where you know there to be animals.

The best way to maximise the chances of meeting a variety of vulnerable road users is simply to do lots of hours on the road.

21 Vehicle Checks

What the learner needs to be able to do

At the very start of their Driving Test the examiner will ask the learner two questions about the safety checks they should make to their vehicle. One will be a 'Show me…' and the other a 'Tell me…' question. There are thirteen possible questions, and these are listed in the AA *Driving Skills Manual*. It is important that the learner driver is sure their vehicle is safe and roadworthy, so they should carry out regular safety checks as standard practice.

How to do it

The AA *Driving Skills Manual* contains detailed instructions on how to carry out the various checks and answer the examiners' questions. If you are using a model of car that is different from the instructor's, you will need to show the learner how these checks should be carried out for that specific vehicle. The learner will need to know how to open and secure the bonnet, as well as how it should be properly closed and checked.

Regular maintenance

It is vital that their vehicle is properly maintained and roadworthy. Not only must they ensure that it is safe to use on the road, but they will be less likely to suffer the inconvenience of a breakdown if they regularly perform a few essential checks.

POWER check

They should carry out this check at least every week, and before any major journey.

Petrol – make sure they have enough for the journey, or at least enough to reach the next petrol station.

Oil – check the engine oil level.

Water – check the levels of the engine coolant and windscreen wash.

Electrics – check all electrical features: lights, horn, indicators, brake lights, windscreen wipers, etc.

Rubber – check the tyres for damage and wear and tear, not forgetting the spare wheel. Also check the windscreen wiper blades for wear, and replace if necessary.

As they perform the POWER check, make replacements or repair any faults you find, and top up any fluid levels as necessary. As they walk around the car, they should check for any damage to the bodywork.

Daily checks

- They should make a visual inspection of the car every day, paying special attention to the tyres, lights and external bodywork, and glass.
- They should walk around the car before getting in for the first time each day. They must check that the tyres are not flat, and that they can see no obvious damage to the tyre walls; make sure the bodywork and glass are intact and check all the lights are working properly.
- Every time they start the engine for the first time that day, they should carry out a brake check – that alone could save their own or someone else's life.

Clean and tidy

Keeping the car clean not only ensures that it is presentable and more pleasant to drive, but will also allow them to spot any potential problems as early as possible. For example, if the wheels are caked in mud, they may not notice the nail sticking in the tread.

They must keep the glass (windscreen, side windows and mirrors) clean at all times – they must always be able to see clearly.

Encourage them to keep the inside of the car tidy, too. They should secure any loose items properly, using the glovebox, door and seat pockets or the boot to safely stow anything they may need to carry. Loose items can become lethal missiles in the event of sudden braking or an accident. They should also make sure that the foot-wells are kept empty, and that they don't store anything under the seats. When they brake, such items could slide forward and prevent proper use of the pedals.

They must make sure any pets are properly secured in the rear of the car. They must not allow them to roam freely around the passenger compartment, as they can distract the driver. For maximum safety, a pet cage or safety bars can be fitted, so that animals are kept separately from the main compartment.

Practice plan

Periodically check that they remember how to perform all the checks. Try to do at least one pair of the real questions (one 'Show me' and one 'Tell me') every time you go out in the car. When practising, get them to do the checks for real – don't just 'tell'. They will find it easier to explain if they have actually performed the checks themselves.

22 Automatics

What the learner needs to be able to do

Whether driving an automatic car or not, they need to know the major differences between automatic and manual transmissions and how to control a vehicle with an automatic gear box. The Theory Test includes many questions relating to the use of automatics.

How to do it

If the learner is taking professional tuition in an automatic car, their instructor will explain all the various controls and methods they will use. If you intend to let them practise in your automatic car, they will need to know the specific details of that car and how it differs from their instructor's car.

It is not a good idea to have the learner taking lessons in an automatic but practising in a manual car. The other way round – learning in a manual and practising in an automatic – is not ideal, but is preferable to having no practice at all.

Automatics allow you to concentrate more on what is happening around you as you will not normally have to change gear. They are ideal for drivers with physical disabilities or the able bodied who drive a high mileage. Many people still believe automatics to be far less economical and lacking in performance, but recent technological advances make modern automatics almost indistinguishable from their manual counterparts.

Common features

Automatic gearboxes come in many different versions, but have some common features. For a thorough understanding of how the gearbox on your car should be used, refer to the manufacturer's handbook.

Vehicles with automatic transmission do not have a clutch pedal. Gears are changed automatically when the car senses a change in speed or load on the engine – for example, going uphill. It is possible to over-ride the sensors and force the car to select a specific gear (so-called 'locked' gears), but for most driving situations the automatic gearbox will select the appropriate gear for the speed at which you are travelling.

The gear selector

Almost all automatics have a gear selector, though there may be minor differences between various models. The layout is usually as follows:

P – Park. This setting locks the transmission and must only be used when the car is stationary.

R – Reverse

N – Neutral. As in a manual gearbox, this setting allows you to have the engine running but with no connection to the wheels.

D – Drive. This setting selects the fully automatic mode. The car will automatically select the best gear for the speed or load on the engine.

3 – third gear (not on all models)

2 – second gear

1 – first gear

The selectable gears 1, 2 and 3 force the transmission to use the selected or a lower gear – the car will not use a higher gear than the one chosen. Use this when going down steep hills, where you would normally use a lower gear.

There may be a lever or switch on the selector itself which you must operate in order to move the selector – check details for your car in the manufacturer's manual.

Creep

Automatics are deliberately designed to 'creep' forward without the need for any pressure on the accelerator. Because of this, it is essential that, when stationary, the learner either keeps their right foot firmly on the brake pedal, or applies the handbrake and selects Neutral. If they stay in Drive, they must have their foot on the footbrake as the handbrake may not hold the vehicle still.

Moving off

Preparation

Most automatics have a cut-off switch which will prevent you from starting the engine while in gear, or unless the footbrake is applied. The learner must know any special procedures that must be used. They should check that the selector is in Park or Neutral and that the handbrake is fully applied when they first enter the vehicle. Before starting the engine, they should press firmly on the foot brake to prevent creep. Once they are ready to move off they should select Drive using the gear selector.

Observation

They must check all around the car, finishing by looking into the blind spot over their right shoulder.

Manoeuvre

They should release the handbrake and then take their foot off the footbrake. The car will creep forward – even on a hill, provided it is not too steep. The car will continue to creep at this speed until they apply some pressure to the gas pedal. If they are performing a manoeuvre such as a turn in the road, they should not use the accelerator, but simply control the speed using the brake pedal. The same applies whether they are going forwards or reversing.

If they intend to drive on normally, as they start to move they should gently squeeze the gas pedal, maintaining a steady pressure as they get to the correct rate of acceleration. The gear box will automatically change up through the gears for them.

Kick-down

If they need to accelerate more quickly – for example when joining a road with a faster speed limit – they can use the 'kick-down' device. This feature, common to all automatics, allows them to over-ride the automatic selection of gears and forces the transmission to stay in the lower gears for longer. This gives them much greater acceleration than normal.

As the name implies, they should press down sharply on the gas pedal. Some models of automatic gearboxes have a definite 'click' on the accelerator pedal when you press down like this, while others just sense the rapid movement and change down for you. The learner should keep the pedal all the way down until they reach the desired speed.

When they reach the speed they want, they should ease back off the gas and the car will automatically return to normal drive and select the most appropriate gear.

Slowing and stopping

To slow down, they must simply transfer their right foot from the gas pedal to the brake. Because of the reduced engine braking, they must brake sooner and more progressively than in a manual car. The transmission will automatically work its way down through the gears as they slow down, so that they are always in the correct gear.

As they come to a stop, they must keep their foot on the footbrake until they have applied the handbrake and are in Neutral.

TIP

The car will not stall as you brake, even if you have stopped very quickly.

Under normal driving conditions they would apply the handbrake whenever a pause becomes a wait. If they are to be stationary for more than a few seconds, remind them to apply the handbrake firmly and select Neutral. If they are parking, they should apply the handbrake and select the Park position before releasing the footbrake.

Additional features

There are a number of situations where the learner may need to use extra features. These include:

- hill starts
- driving downhill
- cornering

- snow or ice
- manoeuvring.

For details of how to deal with all of these siturations, see Chapter 22 in the AA *Driving Skills Manual*. Learners should also be aware of two more additional functions: economy and sports mode.

- Some automatics have an economy mode button which causes the transmission to select the higher gears at lower revs than normal. This saves petrol but at the expense of performance – they will not be able to accelerate as quickly.
- Some automatics have a 'sports' button. In sports mode, the gears will change at much higher revs than normal, giving much more power and acceleration, but at the expense (and I mean expense) of fuel consumption. Sports mode is really only suitable for track days, or occasional use when they need to accelerate quickly.

Practice plan

First steps

Follow the suggestions given in the practice plans for all chapters in the same way, but making the necessary changes to account for the automatic gearbox. Start with simple moving away, stopping and speed control.

Gaining confidence

Practise the use of kick-down and the locked gears when accelerating and going downhill. Experiment with any additional modes available on the car, such as the snow button or economy setting. Practise manoeuvres as they arise in the natural progression of their lessons. They will probably find these much easier than in a manual car.

Ready for the test

Remember that for all the situations detailed in this book where MSM/PSL or other routines are used, they still need to follow the routine – only the specific details of changing or selecting gears will differ. The speed phase of MSM/PSL becomes much easier: the learner should just use the footbrake or gas to get to the appropriate speed. This does not mean that they can delay the MSM/PSL routine when driving an automatic, but it does mean that they are likely to find it easier to control the car, and have more time to concentrate on observations, steering and driving smoothly.

23 The Test

While you may take the learner to their Driving Test, it is most likely that their instructor will take that responsibility. Whatever the case, you should be aware of what they need to take with them, and how the test will be conducted. This will help you in the final practice sessions, when you can plan around their weaknesses or practise specific skills that are most likely to be needed.

If you are going to take the learner to the test, there are many things you need to know. Full details can be found in the AA *Driving Skills Manual*, but the following outline gives the basic requirements.

How to do it

If the candidate can't find any of the required documents listed below, they must telephone the DSA immediately for advice.

Preparation

It is sensible to book a driving lesson for the hour before the test. Make

Legal requirements

Driving Test candidates must take with them both parts of their provisional licence – the photocard and the paper counterpart – and their Theory Test pass certificate. If they have written confirmation of the test appointment it is a good idea to take that too.

If they are taking the test in a private car they should take with them a valid insurance certificate for that vehicle. They must also provide an extra rear view mirror for the examiner's use, and ensure that the passenger seat is secure and has a working seatbelt and head restraint. L-plates must be displayed without obscuring the front or rear windows.

If the weather is very bad on the day of the test, they should telephone the DSA (on 08700 101 372) to check whether tests are going ahead. If the test is cancelled, the candidate will be offered another appointment.

sure the candidate has all the required documents with them, and get them to show them to their instructor before they leave home. If they wear glasses, make sure they have them, too.

They should arrive at the Test Centre at least ten minutes before the appointed test time, to allow time to park and mentally prepare for the test.

The start

The examiner will come out and call their name. The candidate will be asked to read and sign the insurance and residency declarations while the examiner checks that their documents are in order. They will then be asked to lead the way to their vehicle.

Eyesight test

As they walk out, the examiner will ask them to stop somewhere to do the eyesight test. They must be able to read an old-style number plate at a distance of 20.5m or a new-style plate at 20m. If they wear glasses or contact lenses to read the number plate then they must wear them when driving.

At the car

The first part of the test is the vehicle checks, or 'show and tell questions' (see Chapter 21).

The examiner will then usually ask them to get in and prepare. They should get in and perform a brief cockpit drill and put their seatbelt on. When they join the candidate in the car, the examiner will explain what they would like them to do:

'During the test I would like you to follow the road ahead at all times, unless signs or markings indicate otherwise, or I ask you to make a turn, which I will do in good time. When you are ready, drive on.'

This is the candidate's cue to check that the handbrake is on and the gear lever is in neutral before starting the engine.

The test drive

To pass the test, the candidate must commit no more than fifteen driving faults and none of these must be serious or dangerous.

- A driving fault is anything which is not totally correct.
- A serious fault is one which is potentially dangerous and could cause other road users to take action.
- A dangerous fault is one where they cause actual danger to themselves or other road users.

The test will last 35–40 minutes and will cover a variety of roads, including rural and urban roads and dual carriageways. The route will almost certainly include roundabouts, crossroads, pedestrian crossings and roads through residential, shopping and country areas. While every Test Centre has its own character, the routes are planned to include the widest range of driving skills possible and to give a consistent standard of testing across the whole country.

The manoeuvres

During the test the candidate will be asked to perform two of the manoeuvres they have practised. These are chosen from:

- Bay park – this must be done in the Test Centre car park at the very beginning or end of the test.
- Parallel park.
- Reverse into a side road on the left or right.
- Turn in the road.

In addition they may be asked to demonstrate the emergency stop.

On several occasions they will be asked to pull over and park on the left. This may be so that the examiner can give them instructions for one of the exercises, or they may then be asked to move off again immediately.

Navigation

If they come to a junction or roundabout where the examiner has given no instruction to turn, they should follow the road directly ahead. They should always position themselves to follow the road ahead unless the examiner tells them otherwise.

The candidate may ask the examiner to repeat instructions, or question them if unsure. The test is an assessment of the candidate's driving ability, not navigational ability, so they should not worry if they have to ask for confirmation of the directions. If they get confused between left and right, they should ask the examiner to use additional hand signals along with the verbal directions. If they do take a wrong turn, they shouldn't worry, the examiner will simply direct them back to the route or stop them and ask them to turn around.

Suspension of the test

On rare occasions extraordinary circumstances cause the examiner to temporarily suspend the test – for example, broken traffic lights. In such cases the candidate will not be penalised for any faults committed while the test is suspended. When everything is back to normal, the examiner will tell them that they are now testing again.

End of the test

When the candidate has parked back at the Test Centre, the examiner will tell them that is the end of the test. They may take a few moments to complete the form and will then tell the candidate whether they have passed or not.

If they have passed, the examiner will complete the necessary paperwork before offering to de-brief them on their performance. If they have not passed, the examiner will offer a de-brief there and then, and will ask if they would like a form to rebook their test.

TIP

The candidate should ask if their instructor can listen to the de-brief, as they are likely to be either too elated or too dejected to pay much attention to what the examiner has to say.

The examiner will also give them a Test Report Form, which is a copy of the markings, plus a sheet explaining the marks and a guide to the report form.

The national average pass rate is 43% at the time of writing, so if they have passed, they have done well. If they don't pass, don't let them feel too bad – they should just go for it again. If they haven't passed they will certainly need some more tuition before trying again, so make sure they discuss this with their instructor.

Even examiners admit that few people fail because they can't drive well enough. Most fail because of mistakes which are either due to inexperience or nerves or a mixture of both.

Inexperience and nerves can both be improved by practice, so make sure you take the time to give them as much practice as possible.

The Test Report Form and the examiner's de-brief will help you correct their mistakes for the next time, and will also indicate to their instructor how much extra tuition they are likely to need. As a guide, they will need an hour's tuition for every major fault or every five driving errors (minor faults).

If they have not passed, they can book the next test immediately, but they will not be allocated an appointment for at least two weeks.

24 After the Test

Well done! They've passed, and you can claim a good deal of the credit. The examiner decided that they are safe to drive on the roads unaccompanied.

Without detracting in any way from their achievement, please remember that they are inexperienced and probably still not the most skilful driver on the road. Unless they are very careful, statistics show that this is the time they are most likely to have an accident.

Newly qualified drivers are around 10 times more likely to have an accident in the first two years of their driving career than in the whole of the remaining 60 years or so. Two drivers under the age of 25 die every day in crashes in the UK. Twenty per cent of all drivers will crash during their first two years. This is why insurance premiums are so high when they start driving.

Pass Plus

The Pass Plus scheme is designed to help new drivers gain the experience and skills to become a safer driver for life. Supported by participating insurance companies, it aims to enable new drivers to:

- develop their existing skills;
- learn new skills, techniques and knowledge to enhance their driving;
- improve their skills of anticipation and awareness;
- understand how to reduce the risks of having an accident;
- maintain a courteous and considerate attitude when driving.

Pass Plus pupils are encouraged to display green P-plates on their vehicle. Drivers who successfully complete the course are offered substantial discounts on their insurance premiums – usually a free one-year no claims discount. This usually far exceeds the cost of taking the course.

Once they have passed their test, encourage them to talk to their instructor about taking the course.

TIP

Contact the AA Driving School for your local Pass Plus registered instructor.

Motorway driving

Whether or not they take the Pass Plus course, they should consider booking a few hours' tuition in motorway driving. While in theory there is little difference between driving on a motorway or a dual carriageway, those differences are important, and in practice the experience can be quite daunting and intimidating.

The main difference is that there is an extra lane. Another difference is the breakdown procedure. More information on both these topics can be found in the AA *Driving Skills Manual*.

TIP

Rules 248–61 of *The Highway Code* give detailed instructions for the procedures to follow if you break down or are involved in an accident, and rules 249–52 are specific to motorways.

The next step

Having passed their test, they must now take care to drive as they have been taught. They have learnt to drive, maybe to the most basic standard – but what they did to pass their test was the right way to drive, and as a new driver they will now gain experience.

The experience they gain in the first few months is the most valuable they will ever get. This is where, if they let it happen, they will pick up all the bad habits that will stay with them for the rest of their driving career. They must avoid all the bad habits, for they are just that – bad. They have learned the skills that they need to be a safe driver and they have learned the right way to execute those skills. Doing anything other than what they were taught is bad driving.

You can play a major role in helping them avoid bad habits by sitting with them when they drive. Certainly for their first few drives, I would recommend that you sit with them, but don't say anything at all – they have to deal with it on their own. If possible, try to sit with them at other times over the first few months and point out any bad habits that start to appear – drivers seldom notice bad habits themselves, and often prefer to look cool rather than drive well.

While it is unlikely that your learner will appreciate the great service you have done for them until they themselves have to sit in the passenger seat with a learner, you should be proud of your own achievement. Sitting in that passenger seat can be the one of the most frightening experiences of your life. And trying to do it without losing your patience, temper or marbles is a test of even the most resilient characters. So, to you also –

Well done.